IMAGES
of Rail

CENTRAL RAILROAD
OF NEW JERSEY
TERMINAL

ON THE COVER: In the early winter months of 1950, the streamlined *Crusader* locomotives were replaced, in the Reading Shops in Reading, Pennsylvania, by the newer class G-3 Pacific locomotives, which were in return replaced, just a few months later, in June 1950, by FP7 diesels. The FP7 was a 1,500-horsepower diesel locomotive produced between June 1949 and December 1953 by General Motors' Electro-Motive Division (EMD) and General Motors Diesel. This photograph shows the EMD FP7 diesel locomotive No. 905 leading the *Crusader* trainset out of the Central Railroad of New Jersey (CRRNJ) Terminal on Track 7 sometime in 1957. The No. 905 diesel locomotive was retired in 1965. (Courtesy of Underwood Archives.)

IMAGES
of Rail

CENTRAL RAILROAD OF NEW JERSEY TERMINAL

Anthony Puzzilla

ARCADIA
PUBLISHING

Published by Arcadia Publishing
Charleston, South Carolina

Printed in the United States of America

Library of Congress Control Number: 2024930644

For all general information, please contact Arcadia Publishing:
Telephone 843-853-2070
Fax 843-853-0044
E-mail sales@arcadiapublishing.com

Visit us on the Internet at www.arcadiapublishing.com

This book is dedicated to the memory of the late Lori Marie Garth, as well as to Janet Akhtarshenas, and the rest of today's hardworking staff and volunteers at the Liberty State Park. Through their tireless efforts and dedication, the history and legacy of the Central Railroad of New Jersey Terminal are kept alive for railroad historians, visitors, and the next generation of train lovers.

CONTENTS

ACKNOWLEDGMENTS

There are so many wonderful and kind people responsible for making this book possible.

I would like to especially thank Mitchell "Mitch" Dakelman, the president and historian of the Jersey Central Railway Historical Society, who provided me with many photographs from his personal collection. He also wrote the introduction. Special thanks must also go to Erin Rose, a Reference and Digital Projects Archivist with the Center for Railroad Photography and Art who painstakingly provided me with a host of high-resolution photographs, notably from their Donald L. Furler collection. Also, I wish to thank Herbert Harwood Jr., a prolific author and railroad historian; Tom Gallo, president of the Central Railroad of New Jersey Veteran Employees Association; and Frank Reilly, president of the Central Railroad of New Jersey Historical Society, and last but not least Rick Bates, the Archivist with the Reading Company Technical and Historical Society (RCT&HS), for giving me access to photographs from their own personal collections, as well as providing invaluable advice and suggestions to the text.

Thanks to one and all.

INTRODUCTION

Shortly before the writing of this book commenced, I received a letter from author Anthony Puzzilla. He asked me if I could provide him with some images for this book, which tells the story of the Jersey Central's Jersey City Terminal. Since I lived within an hour's drive of Liberty State Park, where the terminal building is located, he also asked me if I could go there and photograph the historic plaques that are displayed there. On a sunny weekend day in May 2023, I did just that. I was lucky to find a parking place, as the park is well-attended. Liberty State Park affords visitors spectacular views of the famed New York City skyline. Finally, he asked if I could write an introduction to this volume. The end result is this piece you are reading now.

"On the banks of the Hudson River, where the water flows by the skyscrapers of New York into the bay, lies the terminal of the Jersey Central Lines. Situated close to Bartholdi's famous statue (Statue of Liberty), it was natural that the railroad should adopt as its emblem, the Lady with the Torch." These are the opening lines to the narration of a documentary film that the railroad made in 1948, commemorating the 100th anniversary of the Central Railroad of New Jersey. That film, *The Big Little Railroad*, was shown to groups when the film was released. After a few years, the five 16mm Kodachrome and optical sound prints that were made were worn out, and the film was discontinued for public viewing.

I first saw this film at a screening at the Canal Museum in Easton, Pennsylvania, in the early 1980s. It was one of two new prints made in 1973 at the request of Bob Hoeft, rules examiner. He asked the railroad's trustee, Mr. Timpany, for funding to make a new copy. Roger Wade, who made the film, stated he suggested two prints to be made. One was sold to the State Railroad Museum of Pennsylvania. The screening was arranged by the late Lantz Metz, who was the curator there, and the late George Hart, who was the curator of the Railroad Museum of Pennsylvania located in Strasburg. So many people came to see the film, it was run twice! That film inspired me to explore the railroad, including the long-abandoned Ashley Planes. A tour of the Ashley Planes, located between Ashley and Mountain Top, Pennsylvania, was conducted in November 1982 and was hosted by Hart. I ventured to Jersey City to see the terminal and yards. Portions of the railroad were still being operated by Conrail and several short lines, but the huge yard in Jersey City had closed with plans to convert it to a world-class park.

The railroad's eastern terminal was located in Jersey City, opposite New York City. It is very close proximately to Ellis Island, where a large complex to process newly arrived immigrants was operated by the federal government in the early 20th century. My great-grandparents and their first four of eight children came to this country from eastern Russia in the 1890s via Ellis Island. Adjacent to Ellis Island is Liberty Island, where the Statue of Liberty is located. They arrived by ferry boat from Ellis Island, which was operated by the United States government from 1892 until 1954 when it closed. Since our family lived near New Brunswick, the few train trips we took into New York were via the Pennsylvania Railroad. However, I would see the Jersey Central yards in Jersey City from the nearby New Jersey Turnpike Hudson River extension. Sometime in 1982, I visited the terminal area. Tower A was still extant, and in the building were papers and ledgers documenting passing trains as well as passing boats that went below the massive Newark Bay Bridge, which was several miles west in Bayonne.

The station itself was left in ruins. It had closed in late April 1967 in favor of rerouting trains into Newark's Penn Station and then taking PATH service into lower Manhattan. After the New Jersey Division of Parks took over the property and converted it into the Liberty State Park, the station was restored, but not all of it. The nearby Bush concrete and steel canopies were in poor condition and fenced off. Despite efforts from a number of groups to restore the sheds, nothing has happened.

During the early years when the station was operated by the National Park Service, a number of programs were held. Under the sponsorship of the Friends of the Liberty State Park, a series of lectures were given in the so-called Blue Comet Auditorium. I was one of a number of speakers who came on a regular basis. My programs included lectures on the CRRNJ, using slides or historical movies of the railroad and of New Jersey. Eventually, when personnel at the terminal changed, the programs were discontinued.

As of this writing in mid-2023, the passengers who pass through the station have little knowledge of the trains that once came in and out of the station. They enter the waiting room, buy tickets for the ferries going to the Statue of Liberty and/or Ellis Island, and leave the station and wait in the long lines to pass through post-9/11 security.

At one time, commuter trains, race train specials, the *Blue Comet*, the *Wall Street*, the *Queen of the Valley*, and the *National Limited* to Saint Louis all operated and the terminal ran 24 hours a day, seven days a week. Nowadays, generally, after the last boat before 5:00 p.m. has left for Ellis and Liberty Islands, the gates are locked, and there is no access to the terminal building.

When Tony asked me to photograph the historical plaques, it was a frustrating experience. Most are behind locked gates or in remote areas not seen by the public, or simply totally inaccessible! It's a matter of personal thought whether the National Park Service is really interested in preserving and teaching about the terminal's colorful history.

Regardless, please step back into the 19th century and enjoy the experience of learning about the Jersey Central's historic Jersey Central Terminal

Mitchell E. Dakelman, President
Jersey Central Chapter of the National Railway Historical Society

One

The Central Railroad of New Jersey Terminal, 1860–1967

In 1860, the Central Railroad Company of New Jersey purchased a waterfront location in Jersey City for its new terminal. Completed four years later, the terminal was constructed with landfill material from New York City and ballast from ocean-going vessels. When the railroad was completed between Elizabethport and Jersey City, following the construction of a mile-long bridge across Newark Bay, its first terminal was a wooden structure that opened on July 29, 1864. By 1889, increased demand required a new terminal, which was to be designed and constructed by the Boston architectural firm of Peabody and Stearns. This was the catalyst for the building of the historic CRRNJ Terminal, which was completed in June 1889, and became fully operational on October 6, 1889. The Baltimore & Ohio Railroad and the Reading Company found tenancy there as well.

With the opening of the Immigration Station on Ellis Island in 1892, traffic increased dramatically. Of the 12 to 17 million immigrants that passed through Ellis Island's Great Hall between 1892 and 1954, approximately two-thirds of these new Americans started their new lives via the CRRNJ Terminal. For many immigrants, the terminal became their Gateway to America. During the peak era of the CRRNJ (1890–1929), between commuters and immigrants, some 30,000 to 50,000 people passed through the terminal daily utilizing 128 ferries. Each day, there were 300 trains in service on 20 tracks and 12 platforms.

Along with its docks and yards, the CRRNJ Terminal was one of several massive terminals that dominated the western waterfront of the New York Harbor from the mid-19th century to the mid-20th century. By 1914, the train and ferry sheds were enlarged to accommodate the growing number of commuters.

Passenger use began to decline with the Great Depression, which started in late 1929. By the end of World War II, competition from other transportation venues hurt railway services. Urban residents moved to the suburbs, cars and buses became the preference of commuters, Hudson River tunnels and bridges picked up traffic, and trucking and air freight for cargo surpassed railway transport. The diversion of trains to Newark via the Aldene Plan was the final nail in the coffin. The CRRNJ filed for final bankruptcy on April 30, 1867, and the terminal was closed.

At the turn of the century, six passenger trains lined up at the original Jersey City Terminal. In 1860, the state gave the CRRNJ permission to extend its line from Elizabethport to the Hudson River in Jersey City. The CRRNJ filled in Communipaw Bay and built this massive terminal. The passenger trains shown in the photograph were operated by the CRRNJ and its tenants: the Baltimore & Ohio Railroad, the Reading Company, and the Lehigh Valley Railroad. (Courtesy of the Library of Congress.)

The CRRNJ Liberty Street Ferry Terminal was located at the foot of Liberty and West Streets in Lower Manhattan. It served as the main CRRNJ's ferry terminal, transporting passengers to its train terminal in Jersey City until 1967. Beginning in the early 1860s, the CRRNJ operated a ferry service from its Jersey City passenger terminal to this ferry terminal. Signs for the Reading Lines and the Baltimore & Ohio can be seen under the façade of the building under the CRRNJ. (Courtesy of New York Public Library Digital Collection.)

An aerial view of the approach to the 1889-built CRRNJ Terminal is shown. The terminal is shown in the forefront of the photograph behind the ferry wharves. The CRRNJ tracks and yards are seen behind the terminal. Additional docks are seen flanking the terminal itself on either side. The terminal, along with its docks and yards, was one of several terminal complexes that dominated the western waterfront of the New York Harbor from the mid-19th to the mid-20th century. (Courtesy of Robert A. Emmons.)

The CRRNJ Terminal in Jersey City also served the Reading Company, Baltimore & Ohio Railroad, and Lehigh Valley Railroad during various periods in its 78 years of operation from 1889 until 1967. This aerial view shows the track side of the terminal with a view of the New York City skyline in Lower Manhattan at the top left portion of the photograph and a segment of Ellis Island seen in the far right of the image. (Courtesy of New York Public Library Digital Collection.)

Beginning in 1892, Ellis Island in New York Harbor was the main immigration facility of the United States. From 1892 until 1924, an estimated 10.5 million people, mostly Europeans, passed through Ellis Island. This aerial view of Ellis Island shows the main building of the complex located on Island One at the top of the photograph. Ferries would transport newly arrived immigrants from their transatlantic steamships harbored in New York Harbor via US Bureau of Immigration cutters. They would head to the wharves located in the front of Island One to begin their processing and screening. (Courtesy of National Park Service, Ellis Island.)

Once immigrants successfully passed inspection and screening, they were allowed to purchase railroad tickets in the railroad room found on the main building's ground floor. Immigrants could buy train tickets from various agents representing the CRRNJ, Pennsylvania Railroad, the Baltimore and Ohio (B&O) Railroad, and others. Beginning in 1904, every railroad maintained a ticket office on Ellis Island. Generally, the railroad ticket agents did a brisk business as only one-third of the immigrants decided to remain in New York City. (Courtesy of the Library of Congress.)

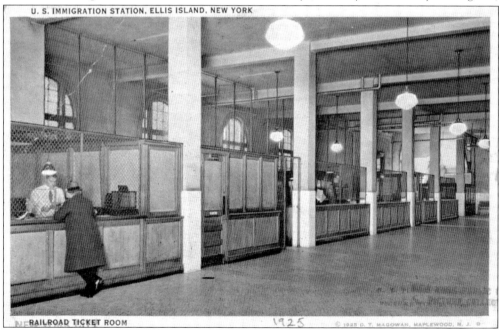

Another view of the railroad ticket room in the main building at Ellis Island can be seen in this 1925 image. The room is not very crowded with customers, as the flow of immigrants from Europe greatly diminished after 1924. (Courtesy of the New York Public Library Digital Collection.)

These immigrants have all gathered to purchase railroad tickets as they begin their new lives in the New World. These tickets were sold by various agents of the nearby rail terminals located along the Hudson River. (Courtesy of author's collection.)

A group of "cleared" immigrants can be seen in the vast waiting room of the main building on Island One at Ellis Island. They are probably awaiting ferry transport from Ellis Island after purchasing their railroad tickets. (Courtesy of the New York Public Library Digital Collection.)

A ferry operated by the US Immigration Service transports immigrants to one of the several railroad terminals located on the Hudson River, or back to New York City for those who decided to find homes in the city itself. (Courtesy of the New York Public Library Digital Collection.)

In this photograph, we can see the relative proximity of Ellis Island and the CRRNJ Terminal Complex. The CRRNJ Terminal offered rail service via the CRRNJ, B&O Railroad, and the Reading Company. (Courtesy of the Library of Congress.)

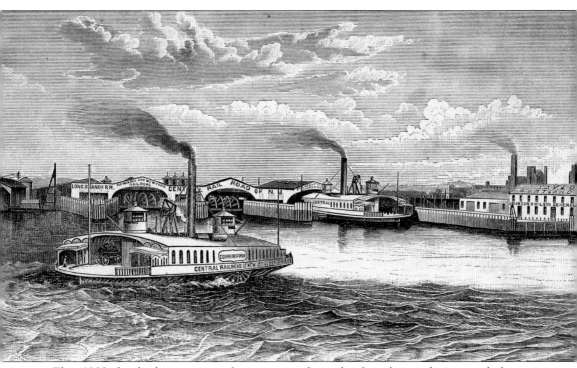

This 1900 sketch shows various ferries approaching the ferry house that covered the entire riverside façade of the terminal. The ferries and barges that brought immigrants from Ellis Island to the terminal would dock inside the ferry house. Immigrants would disembark and be led to the immigrant waiting room within the ferry house. The ferry house was not part of the terminal itself. The immigrants were intentionally kept separate from the terminal's daily commuters. In its heyday between 10,000 and 30,000, commuters passed through the terminal daily. The immigrants were kept clear of the splendor of the main waiting room until the actual arrival of their designated train. Once this happened, they would be escorted by a train official through the north baggage tunnel to the main concourse in order to board their hopefully waiting train. Many of these immigrants had their train tickets pinned to their clothing so that the conductor, and other train officials, did not accidentally have them board the wrong train. (Courtesy of author's collection.)

The blog True Immigrants Tales: After Ellis Island, written by Vince Parillo, recounts a number of actual immigrant stories that appeared in the 1910 report to the Presidential Commission on Immigration: "Finally, we were taken from here to our respective stations. We who were going on the [name deleted] Line crossed in a ferry to a dingy, dirty, unventilated waiting room next to the station in Jersey City. There we waited from 6 o'clock in the evening until after 9. About 8 o'clock, the attendant signaled us to go downstairs, showing our tickets as we went. We were all expected to board the train, so anxiously hurried along, dragging our heavy and numerous hand baggage. The poor, travel-tired women, and the sleepy little children, were pitiful sights. Arrived at the bottom of the long stairs, we waited and waited, but there was no train." In this photograph, immigrants, laden with all their worldly possessions, wait on a train platform for their train to arrive. Often, the train was late, which meant that the immigrants were forced back to the waiting room to once again stay until their train finally arrived. (Courtesy of the Smithsonian Institute.)

WASHINGTON BRANCH AND NEW YORK AND WASHINGTON AIR LINE.

Going South

Station	A.M.	A.M./P.M.	A.M.	A.M.	A.M.		A.M.	A.M.	A.M.	P.M.	P.M.	P.M.	A.M./P.M.	P.M.	P.M.	P.M.	P.M.	P.M.
NEW YORK		9.00											9.00					3.15
PHILADELPHIA		12.40											12.15				4.00	6.00
BALTIMORE	4*20	5*20	6*45	6.50	7.40		8*45	10.00	11.00	‡1.00	3.30	4.00	4.30	5*06	6.00	6.30	8*45	10.30
Relay House	4.38	5.37	7.01	7.08	7.56		9.03	10.20	11.18	1.18	3.48	4.17	4.47	5.24	6.18	6.48	9.02	10.47
Elk Ridge Landing				7.11			9.06		11.21	1.21	3.51			5.27		6.51	9.05	
Hanover				7.17			9.11		11.27	1.27	3.57			5.32		6.56	9.09	
Dorsey's Cut				7.23			9.16		11.33	1.53	4.03			5.37		7.01	9.13	
Jessup's Cut				7.28			9.21		11.38	1.58	4.08			5.42		7.06	9.17	11.06
ANNAPOLIS JUNCT'N	4.36			†7.33			9.26		11.43	1.43	4.13	4.36	†5.06	5.47		7.11	9.21	
Savage				7.37			9.29		11.47	1.47	4.17			5.30		7.14	9.24	
Laurel				7.42			9.34		11.52	1.52	4.22	4.43		5.50		7.19	9.28	
Contee's				7.47			9.39		11.57	1.57	4.27			6.00		7.24	9.32	
Beltsville				7.56			9.46		12.06	2.06	4.36			6.08		7.31	9.37	
Bladensburg				8.12			9.59		12.22	2.22	4.52		5.28	6.13		7.44	9.47	
Metropolitan Junc.				8.26			10.11		12.36	2.36	5.06			6.36		7.56	9.56	
WASHINGTON	5.40	6.30	7.50	8.30	8.40		10.15	11.10	12.40	2.40	5.10	5.15	5.40	6.40	7.20	8.00	10.00	11.40

Going North

Station	A.M.	A.M.	A.M.	A.M.	A.M.	A.M.	M.	P.M.	P.M.	P.M.	P.M.	P.M.	P.M.	P.M.	P.M.	P.M.	P.M.
WASHINGTON	5.00	6*45	8*00	8.45	9.45	10*50	12.00	1.00	2*00	3.30	3.45	4*45	5.45	6.45	7*45	9*3.	9*40
Metropolitan Junc.	5.04	6.49		8.49			12.04		2.04		3.49		5.49	6.49	7.49		9.56
Bladensburg	5.17	7.03		9.20			12.18		2.18		4.03	5.03		7.03	8.01		
Beltsville	5.33	7.20		9.26			12.35		2.35		4.20	5.20		7.20	8.14		10.07
Contee's	5.41	7.29		9.29			12.44		2.44		4.29	5.29		7.29	8.21		
Laurel	5.46	7.34		9.34			12.49		2.49	3.55	4.34	5.34		7.34	8.26		
Savage	5.51	7.39		9.30			12.54		2.54		4.39	5.39		7.39	8.31		
ANNAPOLIS JUNCT'N	5.54	†7.43		9.42			12.58	1.03	2.58		4.43	†5.43		7.43	8.34		10.23
Jessup's Cut	5.59	7.48		9.48			1.03		3.03		4.48	5.48		7.48	8.39		
Dorsey's Cut	6.03	7.53		9.53			1.08		3.08		4.53	5.53		7.53	8.44		
Hanover	6.08	7.58		9.58			1.13		3.13		4.58	5.58		7.58	8.49		
Elk Ridge Landing	6.13	8.03	8.51	10.03			1.18		3.18		5.03	6.03	6.31	8.03	8.54		
Relay	6.16	8.05	8.51	10.06		11.41	1.21	1.56	3.21	4.16	5.06	6.06	6.31	8.06	8.57		10.22
BALTIMORE	6.35	8.26	9.10	10.25	10.31	12.00	1.40	2.15	3.40	4.35	5.25	6.25	6.50	8.25	9.15	10.40	10.42
PHILADELPHIA	11.45		1.30		10.50		6.55			11.30					2.50	11.00	
NEW YORK			4.30			10.08										6.35	

† Connect with trains for Annapolis.   * Run Sundays.   ‡ Leaves at 1.30 on Sundays.

A so-called special "immigration train" was operated by the Baltimore & Ohio Railroad from Track 1 within the CRRNJ Terminal. According to the *Guide to the Baltimore and Ohio Railroad's Washington Branch* timetable, the B&O operated the special train, which left New York at 9:00 p.m. In fact, the B&O had no tunnel rights, so its New York City trains actually originated from the CRRNJ Terminal in Jersey City. The special immigration trains were described as "somewhat resembling cattle cars." The special train made stops in Philadelphia and Baltimore before arriving in Washington, DC, at 6:30 a.m., the next morning. (Courtesy of the National Archives.)

Once the special immigration train arrived at the terminal, and before it left Jersey City, some of the more fortunate immigrants were able to get some sleep aboard the train itself. (Courtesy of National Park Service.)

The B&O Railroad Immigration Train en route to its scheduled destinations south of New York, namely Philadelphia, Baltimore, and Washington, DC. In *True Immigrants Tales: After Ellis Island*, Parillo related this story told by a traveling immigrant: "A trainman guided this weary and dejected party along the car tracks, through the sleet and snow, over an endless distance, it seemed, to the station." Still, another story apparently told by a traveling immigrant: "We were again led to the station to be put on a train. . . . What those immigrants who had to travel longer distances suffered can be well imagined from the experiences of this short journey." (Courtesy of author's collection.)

During the 1940s, a virtual flood of passengers depart a CRRNJ ferry at the Communipaw ferry slip in Jersey City to catch their rush hour trains. Since this routine seems fairly standard in nature, it is assumed that these passengers had no problem locating their designated tracks without further thought or hesitation. (Courtesy of author's collection.)

In March 1954, a number of commuter trains can be seen leaving the CRRNJ Terminal with the New York City skyline in the background. Many former rail passengers preferred driving to work rather than patronizing CRRNJ Terminal–based rail carriers unable to provide direct rail service to downtown Manhattan. The automobile was spreading, the nation's highway system was expanding, and the nearby Verrazzano-Narrows Bridge, constructed in 1964, facilitated commuter transportation within the Metropolitan New York City area. The CRNJ continued running up until its bankruptcy in 1967. (Courtesy of the Herbert H. Harwood Jr. collection.)

This c. 1967 photograph was taken near the end of scheduled passenger service at the CRRNJ Terminal. The dirty Reading Company Rail Diesel Car (RDC) No. 9161 sits on Track 14 in the terminal. This particular track was used by the Raritan Train which provided commuter service to Raritan, New Jersey, and other southern New Jersey locations. This particular RDC was built by the Budd Company of Philadelphia and was delivered to the Reading Company. After the closing of the CRRNJ Terminal, RDC No. 9161 saw service with the Massachusetts Bay Transit and the Winnipesaukee Scenic Railroad. (Courtesy of author's collection.)

Two

The Class I Railroads at the Terminal and Named Trains

For many railroads traveling from the south, the New Jersey waterfront was as close as it would get to the Downtown New York City area of Manhattan. The exception to this barrier was the Pennsylvania Railroad. The opening of the North River Tunnels under the Hudson River and Penn Station in 1910 made the Pennsylvania Railroad the only railroad with direct access to New York City from the south. To reach New York City, railroads either built or shared terminals along the shores of the Hudson River directly opposite Manhattan and used a fleet of ferries to transport passengers directly into the downtown area. These included some of the railroads providing passenger service during the early 20th century.

The CRRNJ Terminal became the New York City origination/destination point for a number of the tenant Class I railroads and their famous named trains. These trains were, and are still today, widely renowned in the annals of American railroading. They included the CRRNJ's *Blue Comet*, the B&O's *Royal Blue*, *National Limited*, *Capitol Limited*, *Columbian*, and *Diplomat*, and the Reading Company's *Crusader* and *Queen of the Valley*.

Baltimore & Ohio trains began using the Jersey City terminal in 1886 via Reading and Jersey Central trackage. During World War I and up until 1926, they were permitted to use Pennsylvania Station in New York City. After that time, they reverted back to using the CRRNJ Terminal in Jersey City again. On April 28, 1958, the B&O passenger service north of Baltimore was terminated. At that time, the *Royal Blue* service was abandoned and the *Capitol Limited*, *Metropolitan Special*, and *National Limited* passenger service was terminated between Jersey City and Chicago, Illinois, as well as between Jersey City and St. Louis, Missouri. For these aforementioned trains, passenger service was therefore cut back to Baltimore or Washington, DC, as their eastern terminals. On May 1, 1971, Amtrak took over most of the nation's inter-city passenger business, including most of the B&O's. A notable exception was their Washington, DC–based commuter operations.

The Liberty State Park has made its own track assignments, as indicated on the departure boards at the CRRNJ Terminal in front of the tracks in the train shed. The Hutchinson train indicators and curtain sign depict the period when the largest number of named trains operated at the CRRNJ Terminal. There, stately metal columns still loom over rows of emptiness where tracks once stood.

Tracks at the Central Railroad of New Jersey Terminal of Named Passenger Trains*

Track No.	Passenger Train	Primary** Operator	Affiliated Operator(s)	Destination	Year Began	Year Ended
1	Royal Blue	B&O	CRRNJ & RDG	Washington, DC	1935	1958
1	Marylander	B&O	CRRNJ & RDG	Washington, DC	1938	1956
4	National Limited	B&O	CRRNJ & RDG	St. Louis, MO via Washington, DC and Cincinnati, OH	1925	1958
4	Capitol Limited	B&O	CRRNJ & RDG	Chicago, Illinois via Washington, DC and Pittsburg, PA	1926	1958
4	Diplomat	B&O	CRRNJ & RDG	St. Louis, MO via Washington, DC and Cincinnati, OH	1930	1958
4	Metropolitan Special	B&O	CRRNJ & RDG	St. Louis, MO via Washington, DC and Cincinnati, OH	1951	1958
4	Columbian	B&O	CRRNJ & RDG	Chicago, IL via Washington, DC and Pittsburg, PA	1931	1958
4	Shenandoah	B&O	CRRNJ & RDG	Chicago, IL via Washington, DC and Pittsburg, PA	1930s	1958
7	Crusader	RDG	CRRNJ	Philadelphia, PA	1937	1967
9	Wall Street	RDG	CRRNJ	Philadelphia, PA	1948	1967
10***	Blue Comet		CRRNJ	Atlantic City, NJ	1929	1941
10	Bullet		CRRNJ	Wilkes-Barre, PA	1929	1931
12	Queen of the Valley	RDG	CRRNJ	Harrisburg, PA	1902	1963
12	Harrisburg	RDG	CRRNJ	Harrisburg, PA	1910	1953
19	Williamsporter	RDG	CRRNJ	Williamsport, PA	1930	1945

*These track assignments are based on research done by others. This includes the following former CRRNJ employees and historians: Bob Hoeft, Tom Gallo and Frank Reilly. When these named trains operated, there may have been times when they were assigned to different tracks other than their designated tracks. However, all efforts were made to keep these trains on their usually designated tracks, so that, as Tom Gallo told me, "patrons could just blindly head to these tracks after they got off their ferries and wade through the crowded concourse" of the terminal. These track assignments may or may not match the existing assignments currently displayed in the train shed at the CRRNJ Terminal at Liberty State Park.

** B&O Baltimore and Ohio
RDG Reading Company
CRRNJ Central Railroad of New Jersey

*** The CRRNJ Blue Comet train was originally assigned to depart from Track 9, but it also could be found leaving on Track 10. For simplicity's sake, it is assigned here to Track 10.

These track assignments are based on research done by others. This includes the following former CRRNJ employees and historians: Bob Hoeft, Tom Gallo, and Frank Reilly. When these named trains operated, there may have been times when they were assigned to different tracks other than their designated tracks. However, all efforts were made to keep these trains on their usually designated tracks, so that, as Tom Gallo said, "patrons could just blindly head to these tracks after they got off their ferries and wade through the crowded concourse" of the terminal. These track assignments may or may not match the existing assignments currently displayed in the train shed at the CRRNJ Terminal at Liberty State Park. (Courtesy of author's collection.)

Table 1 — BALTIMORE AND OHIO ROUTE

WESTWARD — New York to Washington

(to trainside Jersey City)

Station (EASTERN STANDARD TIME)	★11 Metropolitan Special Cars open for occupancy Jersey City 10.00 p.m. Daily			★35 Daily	★27 Royal Blue Daily	★5 Capitol Limited Daily	★1 National Limited Daily	★3 The Diplomat Daily	★523 The Mary-lander Daily
	PM	PM	AM	AM	AM	NOON	PM	PM	PM
Lv New York, N. Y., 42nd St. Station (ROUTE 1) (122 E. 42nd St., opp. Grand Central Term. and Commodore Hotel)	9.55	11.05	12.05	------	8.45	12.00	1.10	3.05	4.10
Vanderbilt Hotel (Park Ave. and 34th St.) (Park Ave. Entrance)	10.00	11.10	12.10	------	8.50	12.05	1.15	3.09	4.15
Wanamaker's (4th Ave. and 8th St.)	10.05			------	8.55	12.10	1.20	3.13	4.20
Columbus Circle Station (Broadway and 59th Street) (ROUTE 2)		11.00		------	8.40	11.55	1.05	3.00	4.05
Hotel Lincoln (8th Ave. and 44th Street)		11.03		------	8.43	11.58	1.07	3.03	4.08
Port Authority Bus Term. (Public Bus Stop, 8th Ave. & 40th St.)		11.05		------	8.45	12.00	1.10	3.05	4.10
Hotel New Yorker (8th Ave. and 34th Street)		11.10		------	8.50	12.05	1.15	3.10	4.15
Rockefeller Center Station (49th St. and Rockefeller Plaza) (ROUTE 3)		11.25		------	8.30	11.50	1.00	2.55	4.00
Hotels Taft, Victoria and Abbey (7th Ave. and 51st St.)		11.30		------	8.35	11.55	1.05	3.00	4.05
Hotel Astor (Broadway and 44th Street)		11.35		------	8.40	12.00	1.10	3.05	4.10
33rd Street Route (Broadway and 33rd St.—33rd St. Entrance) (ROUTE 4)				------	8.45	12.00	1.10	3.10	4.15
Statler Hotel (7th Ave. and 33rd St.—33rd St. Entrance)				------	8.47	12.02	1.12	3.12	4.17
Hotel Governor Clinton (7th Ave. and 31st St.)				------	8.49	12.07	1.14	3.14	4.19
Brooklyn Sta. (371 Jay St. corner Willoughby) (ROUTE 5)		11.00		------	8.45	12.00	1.10	3.10	4.15
Liberty Street Station (C. of N. J.) (Note 1)	10.25	12.01	12.35	------	9.15	12.30	1.40	3.40	4.45
Lv Jersey City Terminal (C. of N. J.) (Note 2)			12.50		9.30	12.45	1.55	3.55	5.00
Elizabeth, N. J. (C. of N. J.)			d 1.08		d 9.46	d 1.01	d 2.11	d 4.11	d 5.16 d
Plainfield, N. J. (C. of N. J.)			d 1.26		d 9.59	d 1.15	d 2.25	d 4.25	d 5.30 d
Wayne Junction, Pa. (Rdg. Co.)			2.54	7.45	10.54	2.10	3.20	5.21	6.25
Ar Philadelphia, Pa. (24th and Chestnut Sts.) (B. & O.)			3.12	8.00	11.09	2.25	3.35	5.36	6.40
Lv Philadelphia, Pa. (24th and Chestnut Sts.)			3.20	8.01	11.10	2.30	3.37	5.37	6.41
Chester, Pa.			----	8.15		2.44			f
Wilmington, Del.			3.52	8.30	11.35	2.58	4.02	6.03	7.06
Newark, Del.			m 4.13	8.45				n 6.16	
Elk Mills				8.52					
Aikin, Md. (Bainbridge) (Note 4)			n 4.38	f 9.15			n 4.30	n 6.34	n
Aberdeen, Md. (U. S. Proving Ground)			f 4.50	9.25		f 3.37		f 6.44	f
Ar Baltimore, Md. (Mt. Royal Station)			5.47	10.04	12.38	4.13	5.11	7.22	8.12
Baltimore, Md. (Camden Station) (Note 3 and 3A)			5.55	10.09	12.43	4.18	5.16	7.27	8.17
Lv Baltimore, Md. (Camden Station) (Note 3 and 3A)			6.10	10.10	12.45	4.20	5.20	7.30	8.18
Ar Washington, D. C. (Union Station)			7.00	10.55	1.30	5.05	6.05	8.15	8.55
			AM	AM	PM	PM	PM	PM	PM

Before it's possible to discuss B&O's named trains operating in and out of the Jersey City or the CRRNJ Terminal, it is necessary to first examine the B&O train schedule issued on January 10, 1954. This particular schedule (Table 1) showed all of the departure times for its named trains originating from the terminal. This schedule also identifies the five different motor coach routes provided by the B&O. (Courtesy of author's collection.)

B&O MAKES IT EASY TO ENTER OR LEAVE NEW YORK . . .

Your Choice of 5 Motor Coach Routes between Trainside and the Heart of New York and Brookly

The convenient way to leave or enter Greater New York is by B&O Motor Coach Train Connection Service. It offers you a choice of 15 places in Manhattan and Brooklyn . . . plus a wonderful view of the famous New York skyline during the short ferry trip across the Hudson River.

Inbound, you step from the train at Jersey City into a waiting motor coach and ride to the station or stop you select—see route maps shown below. Your luggage, checked on the train, is delivered when you leave the motor coach.

Outbound, there is similar service. When you board the B&O motor coach (at the most convenient of the 15 places) you have made your train. This relieves you of luggage handling, long walks or stair climbing as well as Red Cap or taxi service. Enjoy these B&O extra conveniences—your railroad ticket includes this service and there is no other charge.

MOTOR COACH STATIONS: 122 E. 42nd St. (opposite Grand Central Terminal and Hotel Commodore); Columbus

Circle (Broadway and 59th St.); Rockefeller Center (4 Street and Rockefeller Plaza). Brooklyn Station, 371 St., corner Willoughby St.

MOTOR COACH STOPS: Hotels Lincoln, New York Astor, Taft, Victoria, Abbey, Vanderbilt, McAlpin, Sta and Governor Clinton. Also Wanamakers (4th Ave. 8th St.) and Port Authority Bus Terminal (8th Ave. 40th St.).

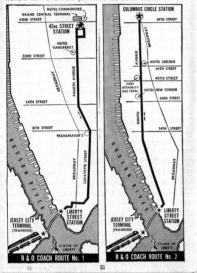
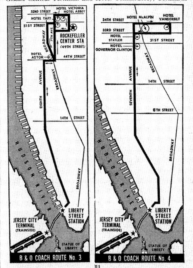

NEW YORK BAGGAGE SERVICE

All B&O Trains Handle Checked Baggage

The B&O provides a special service that relieves you of handling your hand luggage to New York and Brooklyn in train-connection motor coach service. Here are the details:

Inbound Service: Baggage representatives on the train will check your hand luggage to any B&O motor coach station or stop in New York or Brooklyn. And your hand luggage will be carried on the same motor coach with you. If preferred, you may check your hand luggage from starting point to any B&O motor coach station.

Attendants will gladly assist you to transfer hand luggage from 42nd Street Station to Grand Central Terminal, New York City.

Outbound Service: You may check your hand luggage at any B&O motor coach station in New York or Brooklyn in advance or at any time. It will be delivered to your coach seat or Pullman space on the train.

Trunks, theatrical scenery and similar unwieldy pieces cannot be checked to and from motor coach stations and stops. However, these items may be checked to or from Liberty Street Ferry Station or Jersey City Terminal. Baggage Room at Liberty Street Station is open only from 6.30 a. m. to 7.00 p. m. daily.

The schedule also provided a map of these five motor coach routes within the New York City metropolitan area. (Courtesy of author's collection.)

The B&O provided bus service from the CRRNJ Terminal to the heart of New York and Brooklyn via the CRRNJ Liberty Street Station. These buses were loaded onto ferries at the CRRNJ Terminal and then transported across the Hudson River to the Liberty Street Station. The B&O provided motor coach service to and from the Grand Central Terminal and numerous New York City plush hotels and popular tourist sites. These buses provided rail passengers, traveling southbound from the CRRNJ Terminal, convenient trackside service to their waiting adjacent trains utilizing Tracks 2 and 3 within the terminal. There were three generations of stylist Baltimore & Ohio Train Connection Buses that served the CRRNJ Terminal. The first of these buses were the Yellow intercity coaches and the second and third were built and operated by the White Motor Company, commonly called "Whites." An example of the Yellow coaches is shown here lined up in the Jersey City train shed in about 1926. (Courtesy of the Herbert H. Harwood Jr. collection.)

This scene shows second-generation B&O Whites, on Tracks 2 and 3, alongside a B&O train headed by steam engine No. 74 on Track 1 within the CRRNJ Terminal. (Courtesy of the Herbert H. Harwood Jr. collection.)

A B&O Train Connection Special (third-generation White) bus is seen on Track 2 in a photograph taken in the CRRNJ Terminal. It is shown unloading passengers onto a waiting B&O train boarding on Track 1 at the CRRNJ Terminal. It is a late afternoon sometime in 1954. (Courtesy of the Herbert H. Harwood Jr. collection.)

The Camden Station, or Camden Street Station, is a train station at the intersection of South Howard and West Camden Streets in Baltimore, Maryland. Beginning in 1867, and continuing until 1958, it served as the B&O's main passenger terminal and early offices/ headquarters. It was one of the longest continuously operated terminals in the United States. (Courtesy of author's collection.)

B.&O. Feature Trains

Experienced travelers like the smooth, quiet glide of Diesel-Electric power. Today, every Baltimore & Ohio train between New York, Washington, and the West is pulled by a powerful Diesel-Electric locomotive.

Add to this feature those famous "extras" of the B&O — delicious meals, friendly courtesy, and the ability to get there on time — and it is easy to understand why so many prefer to go B&O.

New York—Philadelphia—Baltimore—Washington

The Royal Blue

Diesel-Electric   Air-Conditioned
Reclining Coach-Seats (reserved without extra charge)
Coffee Shoppe   Dining Car   Observation-Lounge
Parlor Car   Stewardess   Public Telephone Service

New York—Washington—Pittsburgh—Chicago

Capitol Limited

Diesel-Electric   Air-Conditioned
All-Pullman between Washington and Chicago
Club Car   Sunroom-Observation-Lounge Car
Train Secretary   Buffet   Dining Car   Radio
(Through sleepers from and to-New York)

The Columbian

Air-Conditioned
Diesel-Electric and De luxe All-Coach Between Washington and Chicago
Reclining Coach-Seats (Reserved without extra charge)
Dining Car   Buffet   Radio
Stewardess-Nurse   Observation-Coach-Lounge Car
(Through Reclining Seat Coaches and Coffee Shoppe from and to New York)

The Shenandoah

Diesel-Electric   Air-Conditioned   Radio
Lounge Car with Buffet   Dining Car   Coffee Shoppe
Through Sleepers, Reclining Seat Coaches
from and to New York
Stewardess-Nurse from Washington

New York—Washington—Cincinnati—Louisville—St.Louis

National Limited

Diesel-Electric   Air-Conditioned   Radio
Coffee Shoppe   Dining Car
Through Sleepers, Reclining Seat Caches
from and to New York
Observation-Lounge, Stewardess-Nurse
from Washington

The Diplomat

Diesel-Electric   Air-Conditioned   Radio
Lounge Car with Buffet   Dining Car   Coffee Shoppe
Through Sleepers, Reclining Seat Coaches
from and to New York
Stewardess-Nurse from Washington

Observation-Lounge on The Royal Blue

20   21

The amenities offered by the B&O trains are presented in this 1947 advertisement. They included diesel-electric locomotives, delicious meals, and courtesy and on-time service. These features were offered on every Baltimore & Ohio train between New York (Jersey City), Washington, DC, and the West. Except for the period from 1917 to 1926, when B&O trains were allowed to use the PRR's Penn Station in New York City, all B&O trains reached the Jersey City Terminal over a combination of Reading Company and New Jersey Central trackage. (Courtesy of Frank Reilly.)

This is a photograph of the Hutchinson train indicator and curtain sign for Track 1 as it currently appears at the CRRNJ Terminal in Jersey City, New Jersey. It announces the *Royal Blue* train leaving the terminal at 9:30 a.m. with service to Philadelphia, Baltimore (Mt. Royal Station and Camden), and Washington, DC (Union Station). Beginning in 1890, the B&O Railroad began what was known as the *Royal Blue Line* between New York and Washington, DC. In 1917, the former *Royal Blue Line* trains were renamed the *Royal Limited*. However, it was not until 1935 that the B&O actually coined the term "*Royal Blue*" as a specific train name. This happened when it first introduced one of its new, lightweight trains operating out of the CRRNJ Terminal. (Courtesy of author's collection.)

The 4-6-4 type No. 2 *Lord Baltimore* steam locomotive was custom-designed by the B&O Railroad, specifically for its new, lightweight version of the *Royal Blue*. The locomotive was custom-built at its Mount Clare Shops. The Mount Clare Shops, located in Baltimore, Maryland, was the oldest railroad manufacturing complex in the United States. It was founded by the B&O in 1829. Mount Clare was the site of many inventions and innovations in railroad technology. It is now the home of the B&O Railroad Museum. When the new *Royal Blue* made its maiden revenue trip on June 24, 1935, it was hauled by the *Lord Baltimore*. Here, the locomotive at the CRNJ Terminal on Track 1 alongside its bus connection at Jersey City in May 1937. (Courtesy of the Herbert H. Harwood Jr. collection.)

The streamliner heads northeast at Ivy City in Washington, DC, in September 1936. A view of the US Capitol Building can be seen in the distance. Ivy City is located in Northeast Washington, DC, and was the home of B&O's rail yard and roundhouse. It served the company's passenger service operations between Baltimore and Washington, DC, at Union Station. (Courtesy of author's collection.)

This is a photograph of the *Royal Blue's* combination parlor-lounge-observation car bringing up the rear on one of its new lightweight trains. (Courtesy of author's collection.)

The parlor-lounge-observation car, aboard the *Royal Blue*, embodied a rather Spartan atmosphere and décor. However, the padded lounge cars look comfortable and inviting. (Courtesy of author's collection.)

As the 1930s dawned, the B&O's New York passenger service faced two significant competitive disadvantages when compared to the Pennsylvania Railroad. First, the B&O lacked direct access to Manhattan, resulting in slower overall travel time. Second, the Pennsylvania's move in the early 1930s to replace steam power with modern, smokeless electric service along its entire New York–Washington mainline was met with enthusiastic public approval. However, it should be pointed out that in the early summer of 1935, the use of diesel power was still only a promising newcomer, and as we have seen, there was also an opportunity to demonstrate steam power's potential on the same type of trains. In August 1935, the B&O began receiving diesel locomotives the EMC (Electro-Motive Corporation) EA units. The diesel locomotive No. 53 is seen here leading the *Royal Blue* train just west of Jersey City, New Jersey, on October 19, 1937. (Courtesy of the Donald W. Furler collection, Center for Railroad Photography and Art.)

The diesel-powered, streamlined, eight-car *Royal Blue* train is seen crossing the famous Thomas Viaduct at Relay, Maryland. The viaduct is one of the oldest stone-arch railroad bridges in the world. The Thomas Viaduct spans the Patapsco River. It was commissioned by the B&O Railroad and built between July 4, 1833, and July 4, 1835, when it was officially opened. It was named for Phillip E. Thomas, the company's first president. (Courtesy of author's collection.)

The B&O was not entirely satisfied with the ride quality of the lightweight *Royal Blue* train. It was replaced on April 25, 1937, with refurbished, heavyweight equipment, a streamlined steam locomotive of the Pacific type designed by Otto Kuhler, painted light gray and royal blue with gold striping. The locomotive is the B&O's "President" class Pacific 4-6-2. The streamlined *Royal Blue* poses at the Thomas Viaduct in this publicity photograph taken in 1937. (Courtesy of author's collection.)

The lunch counter coach provided seating for 14 customers at one time, and lighter fare cuisine than in the more formal dining car. Behind the counter are cupboards and glass racks, and the counter seats were of tubular-frame, satin-finish chromium with blue leather upholstery. A serving kitchen was placed at the end of the lunch counter coach. These cars adjoined each other, and the placement facilitated the preparation and the flow of food between the lunch counter coach and the dining car. (Courtesy of author's collection.)

Sometimes, because of mechanical and/or logistical situations, the B&O would have to mix and match different equipment in order to make a particular passenger service run. In this particular photograph, the *Royal Blue* locomotive 4-6-2 streamlined P-7 class steam locomotive No. 5304 is seen leading the westbound passenger train No. 1, the *National Limited*, at Jersey City on December 10, 1939. (Courtesy of the Donald W. Furler collection, Center for Railroad Photography and Art.)

This is a 1946 photograph of the B&O *Royal Blue* train leaving Track 1 at the Jersey City Terminal with images of Manhattan's skyscrapers in the background. The train's consist is led by the B&O engine No. 51, An EMC EA type diesel locomotive. The EMC EA is an early passenger train-hauling diesel locomotive built from May 16, 1937, to 1938 by the Electro-Motive Corporation of La Grange, Illinois, for the Baltimore & Ohio Railroad. (Courtesy of author's collection.)

The B&O Railroad 4-6-2 P-7 configured engine No. 5314 leads the *Royal Blue* train out of the CRRNJ Terminal with the skyline of Manhattan seen in the right portion of the photograph. This photograph was taken in 1947 on Track 1 of the terminal. (Courtesy of Ed Wittekind.)

THE *Royal Blue*

To expedite service, kindly write your order on check, as our waiters are not permitted to accept verbal orders. Please pay on presentation of your check.

DINNER

| SOUP DU JOUR | MINTED GRAPEFRUIT SEGMENTS | CLAM BROTH |

FRIED MARYLAND OYSTERS, CHILI SAUCE—2.40
BAKED SEASONAL FISH, BUTTER BASTED—2.25
ROAST MARYLAND TURKEY, DRESSING, CRANBERRY JELLY—2.50
BREADED CHOICE PORK CHOPS, SPICY TOMATO SAUCE—2.40
BROILED SELECTED SIRLOIN STEAK—3.90

| CARROTS VICHY | | SOUTHERN STYLE STRING BEANS |
| | CANDIED SWEETS OR HOME FRIED POTATOES | |

| HOT POTATO ROLLS | HOT BREAD SPECIALTY OF THE DAY |

HELP YOURSELF FROM SALAD BOWL

APPLE or PUMPKIN PIE	ICE CREAM	HALF GRAPEFRUIT
BREAD CUSTARD PUDDING	MAPLE BAKED APPLE	
	CHOICE OF CHEESE AND CRACKERS	

| COFFEE | SANKA | POSTUM | TEA |
| | MILK or BUTTERMILK | |

R. O. Mahhee
Manager, Dining Car and
Commissary Department
Baltimore, Maryland

Baltimore and Ohio Dining Car Service

This 1952 *Royal Blue* menu may not be high cuisine in the usual sense of the word, but it featured a number of tasty, favorite regional dishes from the state of Maryland and other Southern delights for the discriminating palette. (Courtesy of author's collection.)

A B&O Railroad *Royal Blue* train is seen highballing around another B&O train in all its artistic glory. (Courtesy of author's collection.)

Also utilizing Track 1 at the CRNJ Terminal was the B&O's *Marylander* train (1938–1956). The *Marylander* was B&O's afternoon passenger train between New York City and Washington, DC. It was operated by the B&O in partnership with the Reading Company and the CRRNJ between Jersey City, New Jersey, and Washington, DC. *The Official Guide of the Railroads* listed the *Marylander* as operating on afternoon schedules in both directions with a 1:00 p.m. departure from Union Station in Washington, DC, and a 5:00 p.m. departure from Jersey City, arriving at its destination approximately four hours later. (Courtesy of author's collection.)

Between the 1930s and its discontinuance in 1956 due to declining patronage, the *Marylander* was equipped with air-conditioned coaches, parlor cars with private drawing rooms, a lounge car, and a full-service dining car, serving complete meals specializing in Chesapeake Bay–style cuisine. Beginning in mid-August 1947, onboard telephone service was provided, making the B&O (along with the Pennsylvania Railroad and the New York Central Railroad) one of the first three railroads in the United States to offer telephone service on its trains. The technology that made this possible was a forerunner of today's cell phones. (Courtesy of author's collection.)

By September 1947, the *Marylander* and all other B&O Railroad New York–Washington bound passenger trains were powered by diesel locomotives. The top photograph shows The Baltimore and Ohio diesel No. 52 with the *Marylander* train at the Jersey City Terminal. They are on Track 1, ready to leave promptly at 5:00 p.m. for Washington, DC (arriving at 8:35 p.m.) with intermediate stops in Philadelphia (6:40 p.m.), Wilmington (7:06 p.m.), and Baltimore's Mt. Royal Station (8:12 p.m.). The photograph on the bottom shows the B&O's diesel engine No. 30 hauling the *Marylander* train No. 525 as it leaves the Jersey City complex sometime in 1954. The skyline of Manhattan is in the background. (Courtesy of the Herbert H. Harwood Jr. collection.)

This photograph shows the B&O's diesel engine No. 30 hauling the *Marylander* train No. 525 as it leaves the Jersey City complex sometime in 1954. The skyline of Manhattan is in the background. (Courtesy of the Herbert H. Harwood Jr. collection.)

Whereas the B&O's named trains *Royal Blue* and the *Marylander* provided passenger service between Jersey City and Washington, DC, there were also a number of the B&O-named trains, which began their respective journeys from Track 4 at the CRRNJ Terminal. They provided air-conditioned, all-Pullman, coach, and full-service luxury dining service for passengers from the Union Station in Washington, DC, to the Midwest cities of St. Louis, Missouri; Chicago, Illinois; and Cincinnati, Ohio. They all provided reclining seat coaches from and to Jersey City and Washington, DC. This service was provided from the early morning hours and throughout the day. This service commenced with trains beginning in 1920. By the late 1950s, all of these trains, as well as most named trains in the United States, suffered steadily declining patronage as the traveling public abandoned trains in favor of airplanes and the automobile. The B&O gave up competing with the Pennsylvania Railroad into New York, discontinuing all passenger service north of Baltimore on April 26, 1958. (Courtesy of author's collection.)

The B&O's premier passenger train between Jersey City and St. Louis, Missouri was the *National Limited*. The train made stops in Washington, DC, and Cincinnati, but avoided the southern Great Lakes, as well as major cities along its route, such as Cleveland and Pittsburgh. B&O's streamlined heyday was in this postwar period, but frugality, smaller stature, and an inconvenient route prevented B&O's trains from challenging the modern cars and ridership of New York Central's *Twentieth Century Limited* and Pennsylvania's *Broadway Limited*. The *National Limited* was introduced on this route on April 26, 1925, as train No. 1 (westbound) and train No. 2 (eastbound). Its inauguration was announced in the May 9, 1925, issue of the *Saturday Evening Post*. (Courtesy of author's collection.)

The *National Limited* was initially all Pullman in the 1920s and 1930s, but coaches were added in the 1940s. Train No. 1 left Jersey City at 12:55 p.m. and arrived in St. Louis the following Noon, allowing passengers to make connections with other railroads. In addition to compartment and drawing-room sleeping cars, the *National Limited* featured a club car, an observation library lounge car, and a full-service dining car. Onboard amenities for the deluxe train's clientele included a secretary, barber, valet, maid, manicure, and shower baths. On April 20, 1932, it became the first long-distance train to be entirely air-conditioned. This photograph shows the B&O Railroad 4-6-2 P-9a steam locomotive No. 5320, the *President Cleveland*, leading westbound passenger train No. 1, the *National Limited*, at Jersey City, New Jersey, on November 8, 1939. (Courtesy of the Donald W. Furler collection, Center for Railroad Photography and Art.)

The *National Limited* traversed some of the most challenging terrain in eastern railroading. It had to assault the Appalachian Mountains in western Maryland and West Virginia in its journey to and from the Midwest. This logistical challenge accelerated the use of diesel power by the B&O Railroad by 1947, in order to provide extra motive power. In this photograph, the B&O's *National Limited* is seen leaving the Jersey City Terminal led by engines E8a No. 91 and a B unit in 1953. (Courtesy of Mitchell Dakelman.)

Sharing Track 4 at the CRRNJ Terminal was the B&O's *Capitol Limited*. Named after the Capitol Building, the *Capitol Limited* was inaugurated on May 12, 1923, as an all-Pullman sleeping car train running from Pennsylvania Station in New York City to Chicago, via Washington, DC. As previously mentioned, on September 1, 1926, the Pennsylvania Railroad terminated its contract with the B&O, which had permitted the latter to use the "Pennsy's" Hudson River tunnels and Pennsylvania Station in Manhattan. Thereafter, the *Capitol Limited*, along with all other B&O passenger trains to New York, operated over the CRRNJ's main line from the connection with the Reading Company in Bound Brook into its Jersey City terminal. From that date until 1958, the *Capitol Limited* became B&O's premier passenger train between Jersey City and the Grand Central Station in Chicago, Illinois, via Union Station in Washington, DC, Baltimore, and Pittsburgh. It was noted for its personalized service and innovation along its entire route. In this 1937 photograph, we see the B&O engine No. 5309 leading the *Capitol Limited* at Roselle Park in New Jersey. (Courtesy of the Donald W. Furler collection, Center for Railroad Photography and Art.)

In 1938, the B&O dieselized the *Capitol Limited* train that ran between Washington, DC, and Chicago, after purchasing two sets of the new EA and EB locomotive units from the Electro-Motive Corporation (EMC). The B&O was heavily in debt during the Depression and could not afford to buy new equipment, so it rebuilt its old heavyweight passenger cars into streamlined ones when the diesels were introduced in 1938, making the *Capitol Limited* the first dieselized streamlined train in the eastern United States. The photograph shows the B&O *Capitol Limited* leaving the Jersey City terminal complex on January 1, 1950. The *Capitol Limited* would end its passenger service at the CRRNJ Terminal in 1958, but it would continue its passenger service between Baltimore and Chicago from 1958 to 1966 and from Washington, DC, and Chicago from 1966 to 1971. (Courtesy of author's collection.)

This photograph, taken on March 20, 1954, at 1:24 p.m. shows a train entering the CRNJ Terminal complex. It is the B&O's *Capitol Limited* train led by the General Motors' EMD E7a73 diesel locomotive. This particular train left the Union Station in Washington, DC, at 9:15 a.m. and was scheduled to arrive at the CRRNJ Terminal in Jersey City at 1:30 p.m., so it looks like it was right on schedule. (Photograph by R.L. Long, courtesy of the National Railway Historical Society [NRHS] Archives.)

While the *National Limited* and *Capitol Limited* were the stars of the B&O passenger fleet between New York (Jersey City) and Chicago and St. Louis, they were supplemented by a number of supporting B&O named trains originating from Track 4 at the CRRNJ Terminal in Jersey City. These other named trains brought B&O's legendary passenger service to small towns across the system, and to passengers who may have been unable, due to scheduling or budget considerations, to ride the flagships of the line. Operating as a running mate to, and carrying overflow traffic for, the crack *National Limited*, the *Diplomat* offered an alternative schedule to that of the *National Limited* run between Jersey City and St. Louis. A number of *Diplomat*'s forerunners operated on this run during the 1920s, but B&O formally named it the *Diplomat Limited* in August 1930. After World War II, the *Diplomat* operated as train No. 3 westbound, and train No. 4 eastbound. This photograph shows the B&O train No. 4, the *Diplomat*, leaving St. Louis, Missouri on September 24, 1935, at about 35 miles per hour. Led by the 4-6-2 engine No. 5222, the train's consist had a total of six cars. (Photograph by Otto C. Perry, courtesy of the Denver Public Library Special Collections.)

An EMD E-7 A diesel engine leads a B&O *Diplomat* train across the picturesque Alleghany Mountains. For its passengers, this was probably the most scenic portion along its route. (Courtesy of author's collection.)

The *Diplomat* train is seen here at Silver Spring, Maryland. The E-7 A diesel engine No. 68 leads the train in this photograph taken in 1947. The *Diplomat* would continue its revenue passenger service to and from the CRRNJ Terminal until 1958. (Courtesy of author's collection.)

This is a photograph of the St. Louis bound B&O *Diplomat* train in the late afternoon of 1954 crossing the long Newark Bay Bridge. According to the B&O train schedule issued on January 10, 1953, train No. 3, the *Diplomat* was scheduled to leave the CRRNJ Terminal daily at 3:55 p.m., and arrive in St. Louis's Union Station in the late afternoon of the following day. (Courtesy of the Herbert H. Harwood Jr. collection.)

The year 1958 was the last for the *Diplomat* train service at the CRRNJ Terminal in Jersey City, although it continued to provide passenger service between Baltimore and St. Louis from 1958 to 1960 and between Cincinnati and St. Louis from 1960 to 1961. It was discontinued on April 30, 1961. In this photograph, the B&O EMD E9A diesel engine No. 1456 can be seen at the CRRNJ Terminal. (Courtesy of author's collection.)

The *Metropolitan Special* operated in daylight between Washington, DC, and Cincinnati, and traveled overnight between Cincinnati and St. Louis. In 1951, the *Metropolitan Special* was extended to become a Jersey City–St. Louis train. Operating on a leisurely schedule, the *Special* served a number of small towns along the B&O St. Louis route, while still providing convenient sleeping-car connections between interim points. Passengers wishing to stay late in the Big Apple could depart on train No. 11 at 12:50 a.m. from the Jersey City terminal, and arrive in Washington, DC, at 7:00 a.m. In contrast to the B&O-named trains, the *Special*'s equipment was older but more comfortable. Dining service was available at some points, sometimes employing full diners and café-club cars, lunch counter cars, or parlor-diner cars. Passenger service between Jersey City and St. Louis lasted from 1951 to 1958, while service between Baltimore and St. Louis was provided from 1958 to 1968, with service between Washington, DC, and St. Louis extending from 1968 until 1971. This painting of the *Metropolitan Special* shows it being led by the B&O EMD E7A diesel engine No. 65 through a picturesque rural setting during the 1950s. (Courtesy of author's collection.)

The B&O's *Columbian* was initially introduced as another competitor to the Pennsylvania Railroad (PRR) in the lucrative New York–Washington, DC, market. In an attempt to further bolster its position, the *Columbian* was refitted, and on May 24, 1931, it made its first run as the nation's first fully air-conditioned train. The following photograph shows the B&O train No. 26, the *Columbian*, as it steams out of Washington, DC, on August 3, 1939. (Photograph by Otto C. Perry, courtesy of the Denver Public Library Special Collections.)

This advertisement was placed by the B&O too promote the *Columbian* running between New York and Washington, DC. Its special features are highlighted. They included a club lounge car, parlor cars, individual seat coaches, a combination observation parlor car, and a colonial-style dining car. Of course, their motor coaches were noted as serving the heart of New York City and its borough, Brooklyn. (Courtesy of Frank Reilly.)

Since the PRR did not operate any streamlined trains between New York and Washington, DC, before the end of World War II, the B&O seized upon this opportunity and quickly began to replace its steam-powered locomotive-led trains with diesel-powered streamlined trains in this market. This photograph shows the B&O diesel locomotive No. 53 with the *Columbian* passenger train traveling eastbound in Jersey City, New Jersey, on October 7, 1939. (Courtesy of the Donald W. Furler collection, Center for Railroad Photography and Art.)

In May 1949, the *Columbian* train was completely re-equipped with streamlined lightweight cars, including a single-strata dome coach lounge. It was among the first dome cars introduced in the East. The PRR was unable to introduce dome cars on their trains due to the height restrictions imposed by their Hudson River tunnels into New York City. This photograph shows the *Columbian* at the Thomas Viaduct sporting its new Strata-Dome coach. (Courtesy of author's collection.)

DINING CAR — The Columbian, B & O Strata-Dome Coach Streamliner

After the PRR successfully introduced the streamlined *Trial Blazer* as a luxury all-coach train in the New York–Washington–Chicago market in 1939, the B&O rebuilt the Columbian and in December 1941 moved it from the New York to Washington run to be a primarily Washington to Chicago train. Another feature of the *Columbian* train was its exquisite dining car. It offered delicious meals in a rather modest but cheerful surrounding. (Courtesy of author's collection.)

Bringing up the rear of the *Columbian* was the observation-buffet-lounge car. This is a photograph of the "Chicago," which made the New York–Washington–Chicago circuit for the B&O, although the observation car only operated on the Washington to Chicago portion of the trip. By the way, the "Chicago" survives today at the B&O Railroad Museum in Baltimore, Maryland. (Courtesy of author's collection.)

OBSERVATION LOUNGE — The Columbian, B & O Strata-Dome Coach Streamliner

The interior of the *Columbian's* observation-buffet-lounge car can be seen in this postcard which shows the observation lounge car aboard the *Columbian's* Strata-Dome coach Streamliner. (Courtesy of author's collection.)

The *Shenandoah* was one of three B&O trains operating between Jersey City, New Jersey, and the Grand Central Station in Chicago via Washington, DC, and Pittsburgh from the 1920s to the 1950s. The other previously discussed B&O-named trains of that period were the *Capitol Limited* and the *Columbian*. The *Shenandoah* offered a late afternoon train (train No. 7 departing at 6:45 p.m.) from Jersey City to Washington, DC. It then provided a very late-evening departure from Washington, DC (11:59 p.m.) with an early morning arrival in Pittsburgh (7:25 a.m.). Continuing westward, the train became a day train between Pittsburgh and Chicago (arriving at 4:25 p.m.). Eastbound, the train offered a late-night departure from Chicago (train No. 8 departing at 10:15 p.m.), assuring a scenic daylight ride through the picturesque Alleghenies. The following photograph shows the *Shenandoah* being led by steam locomotive No. 5066 near Washington, DC, on September 29, 1937. The locomotive is pulling seven Pullman cars. (Courtesy of author's collection.)

The *Shenandoah* became dieselized during the 1940s and streamlined. Its late afternoon arrival schedule in Chicago made it a favorite of travelers seeking convenient connections with other railroads in Chicago, including the streamliners of the Santa Fe and Union Pacific Railroads. A dining and parlor car were provided on the Jersey City to Washington, DC, segment of the trip with passenger cars equipped with roomettes provided on the Washington, DC, to Chicago segment. The train also carried a heavy volume of mail and express, with "head-end" equipment, such as railway post office cars, becoming a standard part of the *Shenandoah*'s consist on its Washington, DC-to-Chicago segment. Beginning on January 16, 1954, the train included a transcontinental sleeping car from Washington, DC, continuing past Chicago on the Santa Fe Railway's *Super Chief*. The *Shenandoah* provided passenger service between Jersey City and Chicago until 1958, although service between Baltimore and Chicago continued from 1958 until 1962, while passenger service between Washington, DC, and Chicago lasted from 1962 through 1971. This photograph shows the E8A diesel engine No. 30 as it leads the *Shenandoah* train out of Jersey City on June 18, 1954, with the skyline of New York City in the background to the right. (Courtesy of M. Cusick.)

Between 1937 and 1967, the *Crusader* provided passenger service for Reading at the CRRNJ Terminal. It was a five-car stainless steel streamlined express train that ran on a 90.3-mile route from Philadelphia to Jersey City's CRRNJ Terminal, with ferry connections to Lower Manhattan at 23rd and Liberty Streets. Built by the Budd Company of Philadelphia, the train consisted of two stainless-steel coaches, two observation cars, and a tavern-dining car or cocktail lounge car on the marquee. Each end had a round-end observation car, a coach adjacent, and the tavern car in the middle. (Courtesy of author's collection.)

The train received its name thanks to a contest that offered $250 to the winning entry, which was selected by a committee of 29 railroad officials. A total of 6,086 entries were submitted, and the person who suggested "Crusader" as the name was P.W. Silzer of Plainfield, New Jersey. Perhaps Silzer was thinking of an image of the fabled Crusader knight when he coined the name of the train for the contest. (Courtesy of author's collection.)

SCHEDULE—Stainless Steel Streamlined Train

Effective December 13, 1937

EASTBOUND	Mondays to Fridays incl. A.M.	P.M.	Saturdays only A.M.	P.M.	WESTBOUND	Mondays to Fridays incl. A.M.	P.M.	Saturdays only A.M.	P.M.
Lv. Philadelphia					Lv. New York				
" Reading Terminal.......	7.40	2.00	7.00	2.00	" Liberty Street..........	10.00	5.30	10.00	5.00
" North Broad Street.....	7.46	2.06	7.06	2.06	" W. 23rd Street..........	9.45	5.15	9.45	4.45
" Wayne Junction.......	7.51	2.11	7.11	2.11	" Elizabeth	b10.27	...	b10.27	b5.27
" Jenkintown	7.59	2.19	7.19	2.19	" Plainfield	b10.40	...	b10.40	...
" West Trenton..........	...	2.39	7.39	2.39	" West Trenton..........	11.12	...	11.12	6.14
" Plainfield	...	b3.10	...	b3.10	" Jenkintown	11.31	6.57	11.31	6.35
" Elizabeth	...	b3.22	...	b3.22	" Wayne Junction........	11.39	7.05	11.39	6.44
Ar. New York (W. 23rd St.).	9.42	4.02	9.07	4.02	" North Broad Street.....	11.43	7.09	11.43	6.48
" New York (Liberty St.).	9.25	3.50	8.50	3.50	Ar. Reading Terminal......	11.50	7.15	11.50	6.55

Consult regular timetables for detailed schedules and complete Philadelphia-New York service.
b—*Stops on notice to Agent or Conductor to take on or let off passengers for or from Reading Co. points.*

Typical Fares between Philadelphia and New York......$1.80   Wayne Junction and New York......$1.70
Jenkintown and New York....$1.65   Philadelphia and Elizabeth....$1.55   Jenkintown and Plainfield....$1.15

$250⁰⁰ *for a Name* suitable for this STAINLESS STEEL STREAM-LINED TRAIN. The Reading Company will pay an award of $250.00 in cash to the through patron of this train who submits the accepted name.

The Reading Company promoted the *Crusader* as the "world's most modern train." The train was noted for its streamlined appearance and stainless steel construction. The train made a "special introductory run" from Philadelphia to Hershey, Pennsylvania on Monday, November 29, 1937. More than 150 people were passengers on the train's first run. In this photograph, the Reading Company 4-6-2 streamlined steam locomotive No. 118 is pulling westbound passenger train No. 607, the *Crusader*, at Jersey City, New Jersey, on September 13, 1939. (Courtesy of the Donald W. Furler collection, Center for Railroad Photography and Art.)

The photograph shows a group of ferry stations occupied by the CRRNJ, Reading Company, and others at the foot of West Twenty-Third Street in New York City. This was one of two ferry terminals used by the CRRNJ and Reading in order to transport their passengers from lower Manhattan to the CRRNJ Terminal in Jersey City. The other ferry terminal was located at the previously discussed Liberty Street. Generally, passengers would be loaded onto ferries at this location first before proceeding to the CRRNJ's main ferry terminal on Liberty Street. The Reading Railroad utilized these ferries in order to transport its rail passengers for the *Crusader* and their other named trains. The Twenty-Third Street ferry terminal remained in existence until 1947. (Courtesy of author's collection.)

The *Crusader* consist included a dining car where delicious meals, prepared in the kitchen, were served. The meals were considered economical and numerous waiters were there to promptly serve each and every passenger. The popular cocktail lounge car was the rendezvous site for business or pleasure. Each of the passenger coaches was provided with a smoking lounge furnished with comfortable armchairs. This photograph shows the Reading Company 4-6-2 streamlined steam locomotive No. 117 pulling eastbound passenger train No. 636, the *Crusader*, at Jersey City, New Jersey, on October 18, 1939. (Courtesy of the Donald W. Furler collection, Center for Railroad Photography and Art.)

Perhaps the most popular car on the *Crusader* was the observation lounge car, especially the rear one. They were richly furnished with deeply upholstered armchairs. Through its broad, clear windows, the passengers could view the flying panorama of the beautiful countryside, read, or talk to others in leisure and comfort. This photograph shows the Reading Company 4-6-2 streamlined steam locomotive No. 117 pulling westbound passenger train no. 607, the *Crusader*, at Jersey City, New Jersey, on November 3, 1939. (Courtesy of the Donald W. Furler collection, Center for Railroad Photography and Art.)

Even though the stainless-steel shrouded streamlined Pacific-class (4-6-2) steam locomotives were prominently used to power the *Crusader* train, beginning in 1937, the older steam locomotives were occasionally substituted due to mechanical or logistical situations. In this photograph, the Reading Company 4-6-2 steam locomotive No. 178 is seen pulling eastbound train No. 636, the *Crusader*, at Jersey City, New Jersey on November 17, 1939. (Courtesy of the Donald W. Furler collection, Center for Railroad Photography and Art.)

The Reading Company's *Crusader* 4-6-2 class G1-sa Pacific locomotive No. 117 stops at a crossing in order to allow people to cross the tracks. The No. 117 was built in 1918 at the Reading Shops. It was worth stopping in your tracks in order to admire the unique design and revolutionary technology the 1930s Art Deco train brought to railroading. (Courtesy of author's collection.)

Track 9 at the CRRNJ Terminal was the home of an additional Reading Company–named train, the *Wall Street*. The CRRNJ's famed *Blue Comet* train was housed there as well. For the sake of simplicity, and the fact that the *Blue Comet* is already regaled on Track 10 at the CRRNJ in Liberty State Park, we will discuss the *Blue Comet* later in this book when we get to that particular track. The *Wall Street* train provided air-conditioned passenger service between Jersey City and Philadelphia between the years 1948 and 1967. When the *Wall Street* made its debut in 1948, it typically departed the Jersey City Terminal at about 4:45 p.m. However, in the mid-1950s, the *Wall Street* departed the terminal at 5:42 p.m. and made six interim stops, including West Trenton, New Jersey, before arriving at the Reading Terminal in Philadelphia. A cocktail lounge car was always included in the train's consist so tired business people could unwind on their way home from work in New York City. (Courtesy of author's collection.)

The marquee in the CRRNJ train shed also shows the Reading Company's *Philadelphia Express* as departing from Track 9. However, according to Rick Bates, the Archivist with the RCT&HT, this is misleading. According to him, "the name *Philadelphia Express* does not appear in any of the Reading Company's timetables in the 1930s through 1960s." He suggests that the confusion might be that all unnamed Reading Company trains, like train No. 1613, traveling from Jersey City to Philadelphia were considered as "expresses to Philadelphia" hence the use of this name on the marquee. The following photograph shows the Pacific G-3 steam locomotive No. 210 leading the *Wall Street* train No. 619 at Bound Brook, New Jersey. (Courtesy of the John Krause collection.)

Here is another photograph of the Reading Company 4-6-2 Pacific G-3 steam locomotive No. 210. This time it is seen pulling train No. 602, the *Wall Street*, at Middlesex, New Jersey on March 25, 1948. (Courtesy of the Robert Morris collection.)

TRACK 10   TRACK 10

10-13 A.M.

THE
BLUE COMET

RED BANK
LAKEWOOD
LAKEHURST
HAMMONTON
EGG HARBOR
ATLANTIC CITY

CHANGE AT LAKEWOOD FOR
TOM'S RIVER
BEACHWOOD
PINEWALD
FORKED RIVER
BARNEGAT

DINING CAR
ATTACHED TO
THIS TRAIN

Probably the most famous named train ever to have its home at the CRRNJ Terminal was the CRRNJ's *Blue Comet*. Often referred to as the "Seashore's Finest Train," The *Blue Comet* was the brainchild of R.B. White, the CRRNJ's president in 1928. Inspired by the *Playground Special*, he envisioned this train would whisk all classes of passengers from Jersey City to Atlantic City in about three hours. Unlike the Pennsylvania Railroad's *Atlantic City Limited* and *New York Limited* service, everyone would enjoy luxury accommodations at regular coach fare. Although photographic evidence clearly shows that the *Blue Comet* operated from Track 9 within the CRRNJ Terminal, we shall acquiesce to the decision of the Liberty State Park people and assign it to Track 10 instead. There were three factors behind the creation of the *Blue Comet*: to eliminate passenger service south of Winslow Junction, to replace rail service with bus connections to better compete with the Pennsylvania Railroad (PRR) for Atlantic City passengers, and to eliminate a costly Pullman parlor car lease. (Courtesy of author's collection.)

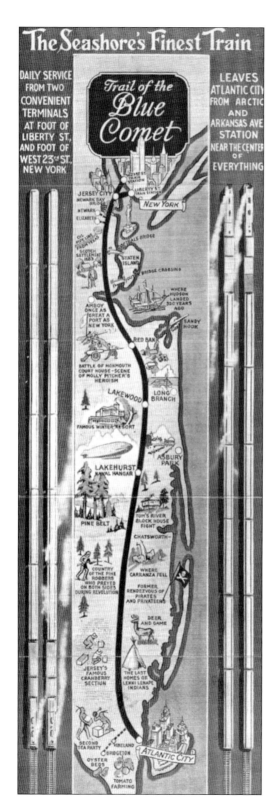

The route selected for the *Blue Comet* passed through a number of historical and picturesque locations in the state of New Jersey, such as the Naval Air Station Lakehurst, the Pine Belt, and so many more before reaching Atlantic City with its multitude and myriad of attractions, shows, sights, and delights. (Courtesy of Robert A. Emmons.)

THE BLUE COMET

THE SEASHORES FINEST TRAIN

—Magnificent, Beautiful, Colorful
—Like a Mighty Meteor Flashing in the Heavens—It Bursts Across the Railway Firmament and Takes a Unique, Commanding Place in the Eyes of the Country.

De Luxe Coach Train between
New York and Atlantic City

3 Hours Flat New York and Atlantic City!

Speed without Excess Fare!
Velvet Smoothness with Roller Bearings!
Safety with Automatic Train Control!
Every Car Named After a Comet!

Individual Seats — Triple Cushioned!

Special Lounge for Ladies!
Special Baggage Attendants!
Unique Smoking Car!

Observation Car — 50 De Luxe Chairs!

ALL FOR COACH PASSENGERS AT THE STANDARD COACH FARE!

APPETIZING 75c MEALS

ALSO $1.25 DINNER

A Dining Car of the modern type, seating thirty-six people, is operated on the BLUE COMET, leaving New York at 11.00 a.m. and Atlantic City at 4.35 p.m. Appetizing meals skillfully prepared and served . . . at moderate cost. Also a la carte service.

SCHEDULES IN EFFECT FEBRUARY 21, 1929

Daily	Daily	TRAIN STATIONS	Daily	Except Sunday	Sunday Only
3.17 pm	10.47 am	Lv N. Y. West 23d Street . . . . . Ar	12.27 pm	7.47 pm	8.42 pm
3.30 pm	11.00 am	Lv N. Y. Liberty Street . . Ar	12.15 pm	7.35 pm	8.30 pm
3.42 pm	11.13 am	Lv Jersey City Terminal. . Ar	12.03 pm	7.23 pm	8.18 pm
*3.57 pm	*11.28 am	Lv Elizabethport (See Note).Ar	*11.47 am	*7.08 pm	*8.02 pm
*4.34 pm	*12.06 pm	Lv Red Bank . . . . Ar	*11.08 am	*6.30 pm	*7.23 pm
6.30 pm	2.00 pm	Ar Atlantic City Lv	9.15 am	4.35 pm	5.30 pm

Note: Newark: Direct connecting train—leaves 15 minutes earlier, and arrives 15 minutes later. *Stops only to receive or discharge passengers.

WALTER V. SHIPLEY
PASSENGER TRAFFIC MANAGER

B. D. BRANCH
GENERAL PASSENGER AGENT

H. E. SIMPSON
ASST. GENERAL PASSENGER AGENT

CENTRAL RAILROAD OF NEW JERSEY — 143 Liberty Street, New York

PRINTED IN U. S. A.

POOLE BROS. INC., CHICAGO

The interior of a color brochure published by CRRNJ provided illustrative information regarding all aspects of the *Blue Comet*, including a description of its unique consist, its luxurious and comfortable accommodations coaches and attentive personnel, its easy riding, and its cleanliness. (Courtesy of Robert A. Emmons.)

In this publicity photograph, a group of visitors are exiting a *Blue Comet* observation car during a tour of the *Blue Comet* equipment held at the CRRNJ Terminal on February 14, 1929. The porter dressed in the *Blue Comet* French blue uniform is probably James S. McKennan. The special blue uniforms worn by the porters were made at the well-known Sigmund Eisner factory in Red Bank, New Jersey. (Courtesy of Joel Rosenbaum and Tom Gallo.)

The *Blue Comet* is seen on its publicity run at Red Bank, New Jersey, on Saturday, February 17, 1929, four days before the start of its revenue service. The festivities at Red Bank were covered in detail by the *Red Bank Register* of Wednesday, February 20, 1929. The title of the article was "The Comet's New Trail." The article noted that "the third largest gathering ever at the Red Bank railroad depot was there Sunday morning to greet the Central Railroad's *Blue Comet*, which is to be the seashore's finest train." The article noted that nearly 3,000 people turned out on the platform to see the train. (Courtesy of Joel Rosenbaum and Tom Gallo.)

The *Blue Comet* is "staged" for still another CRRNJ publicity photograph. The locomotive No. 831 is shown heading up this set of equipment. This same photograph was used in advertisements for seats used on the *Blue Comet*, roller bearings, and a colorized pocket calendar. This photograph can be seen hanging at the Clinton Station Diner in Clinton, New Jersey. Initially, the CRRNJ refurnished 13 cars for the two round trips. Two coaches and an observation car were added later. A typical *Blue Comet* train would consist of a baggage car, a combine smoker, coaches, a diner, and an observation car. The colors chosen for the *Blue Comet* cars were Packard blue, which represented the sky; Jersey cream, for the sandy coastal beaches; and royal blue, for the sea. (Courtesy of Joel Rosenbaum and Tom Gallo.)

At long last, after the completion of its publicity runs and photograph opportunities, the *Blue Comet* was finally inaugurated on February 21, 1929. Following its first arrival in Atlantic City, a formal dinner was held for railroad officials at the magnificent Hotel Dennis. This photograph shows the *Blue Comet* leaving the CRRNJ Terminal in 1938, led by locomotive No. 832. Initially, two brand new Baldwin G-3 Pacific locomotives, No. 831 and No. 832, were assigned to the train. A third G-3 No. 833 would be added later. (Courtesy of the Herbert H. Harwood Jr. collection.)

NEW YORK—LAKEWOOD—LAKEHURST—ATLANTIC CITY

TABLE 1

EASTERN STANDARD TIME — WEEK-DAYS—SOUTHBOUND — SUNDAYS—SOUTHBOUND

For Daylight Time Add One Hour STATIONS	Miles	3303 4201	4205	4203	4209 (SATURDAYS ONLY)	4211	4215	4217	4229			4251	4257	4253	4261	4255	338 45(
Leave		AM	AM	AM	AM	PM	PM	PM	PM			AM	AM	AM	PM	PM	P
New York, West 23d Street	....	....	8.47	9.47	11.45	12.07	2.17	2.25	3.45	....	....	6.47	8.47	9.47	1.15	2.17	7.
New York, Liberty Street	....	2.30	9.00	10.00	12.00	12.30	2.30	2.40	4.05	....	....	7.10	9.00	10.00	1.30	2.30	8.
Jersey City	1.0	2.52	9.12	10.13	12.13	12.42	2.42	2.52	4.17	....	....	7.22	9.12	10.13	1.42	2.42	8.
Jackson Avenue ... Leave	....	....	9.18	▲9.43	▲11.41	12.48	▲2.26	▲2.26	▲3.37	....	....	7.29	9.18	§9.27	▲1.10	▲2.10	8.
Newark, Broad Street ... Leave	....	....	9.05	10.12	11.54	12.42	2.40	2.45	4.15	....	....	7.24	9.07	10.12	1.33	2.40	8.
Newark Transfer ... Leave	....	....	....	....	....	12.54	....	....	....	....	....	7.36	....	....	....	....	...
Elizabeth ... Leave	....	3.05	9.15	10.13	12.03	12.39	2.35	2.35	4.15	....	....	7.08	9.25	10.03	1.29	2.31	8.
Elizabethport ... Leave	10.6	3.19	9.32	★10.28	a12.28	1.06	★2.57	a3.07	a4.32	....	....	7.48	9.34	★10.28	a1.57	★2.57	8.
Perth Amboy	22.1	3.54	9.50	....	....	1.30	....	....	....	....	....	8.18	....	....	....	....	8.
Matawan	29.5	4.30	....	....	....	1.51	....	....	....	....	....	8.33	....	....	....	....	9.
Red Bank ... Leave	39.4	5.46	10.15	★11.04	1.10	2.16	★3.32	3.48	5.13	....	....	8.52	10.13	★11.04	2.39	★3.32	9.
Shrewsbury	41.1	5.52	....	Dining Car	....	2.27	....	....	....	....	....	....	....	Dining Car	....	....	f9.
Eatontown	42.7	5.57	....		....	2.30	....	....	5.20	....	....	8.59	....		....	....	9.
Shark River	48.6	f6.08	....		....	f2.39	....	....	f5.34	....	....	f9.08	....		....	....	f9.
Farmingdale	52.1	6.17	10.32		1.28	2.46	....	....	5.41	....	....	9.15	10.32		2.56	....	9.
Maxim	54.8	6.23	....		....	....	....	....	f5.45	....	....	f9.19	....		....	....	10 f
Lakewood ... Arrive	59.3	6.30	10.46		1.41	3.02	....	4.15	5.54	....	....	9.26	10.44		3.08	....	10.
Lakewood ... Leave	59.3	6.48	10.46	★11.29	1.41	3.02	★3.57	4.15	5.54	....	....	9.26	10.44	★11.29	3.08	★3.57	10.
South Lakewood	62.8	f6.55	....	....	....	3.09	....	....	f6.00	....	....	f9.32	f10.51	....	....	....	10 f
Lakehurst ... Arrive	67.2	7.06	11.00	....	1.54	3.16	....	4.29	6.05	....	....	9.47	10.58	....	3.19	....	10.
Lakehurst ... Leave	67.2	7.06		★11.41	....	3.21	★4.08		....	....	....	....		★11.41		★4.08	
Whitings	73.0	7.22			....	3.31			....	....	....	....					
Pasadena	77.7	f7.27			....	f3.36			....	....	....	....					
Woodmansie	80.5	f7.33			....	f3.41			....	....	....	....					
Chatsworth	85.6	7.40	Parlor Car	The Blue Comet	Parlor Car Dining-Club Car	3.48	The Blue Comet	Parlor Car	....	....	....	....	Parlor Car	The Blue Comet	Parlor Car	The Blue Comet	
Pine Crest (Harris)	88.4	f7.44			....	f3.52			....	....	....	....					
Sandy Ridge	91.0	f7.48			....	f3.56			....	....	....	....					
Atsion	96.8	7.55			....	4.03			....	....	....	....					
Parkdale	99.2	f7.57			....	f4.08			....	....	....	....					
Elm	103.8	f8.06			....	f4.20			....	....	....	....					
Winslow Junction ... Arrive	105.3	8.10			....	4.23			....	....	....	....					
Winslow Junction ... Leave	105.3	⊕8.39	....	....	....	⊕5.16	....	....	....	....	....	....	....	....	....	....	
Hammonton	108.3	⊕8.45	....	12.29	....	⊕5.22	4.59	....	....	....	....	....	....	12.29	....	4.59	
Egg Harbor	119.4	⊕9.05	....	....	....	⊕5.40	δ5.28	....	....	....	....	....	....	....	....	δ5.22	
Atlantic City (Atlantic and Arkansas Aves.) Arrive	136.3	⊕9.30	....	1.00	....	⊕6.06	5.30	....	....	....	....	....	....	1.00	....	5.30	
		AM	AM	PM	PM	PM	PM	PM	PM			AM	AM	PM	PM	PM	PM

No Baggage Carried

Passengers for stations Shrewsbury to

EXPLANATION OF REFERENCE MARKS

a—Stops on notice to Agents to take passengers.
b—Stops on notice to Conductor to leave passengers.
f—Stops on notice to Agent to take passengers and on notice to Conductor to leave passengers.

★—Stops only on notice to Agent to take passengers for Hammonton and points beyond.

The southbound segment (New York to Atlantic City) of the CRRNJ's May 26, 1929, timetable is shown. The timetable shows both the regular local rail service, as well as the *Blue Comet* train service. Note that the timetable cleverly denotes the *Blue Comet* trains by the use of the streaking *Blue Comet* logo. The two daily *Blue Comet* southbound trains to Atlantic City were numbered 4203 and 4213. On Sundays, they were numbered 4253 and 4255. A dining car was provided only on trains No. 4203 and No. 4253. (Courtesy of Joel Rosenbaum and Tom Gallo.)

The *Plainfield* was one of the CRRNJ's ferries, which transported both passengers and vehicles from lower Manhattan, across the Hudson River, to the railroad's massive terminal in Jersey City. These ferries serviced both of the CRRNJ's Liberty Street and Twenty-Third Street terminals. These ferry operations were a vital and indispensable part of CRRNJ's operations since there was no direct rail link to lower Manhattan. Other notable named CRRNJ ferries were the *Westfield* and the *Elizabeth*. At its busiest, more than 200 ferry sailings transported tens of thousands of commuters and thousands of immigrants over the New York Harbor waters. (Courtesy of author's collection.)

On Sunday, November 13, 1938, the southbound *Blue Comet* to Atlantic City is seen making a station stop at Lakehurst, New Jersey. Its consist includes eight cars headed by Pacific No. 832. By this time in its service run, the *Blue Comet* consist was not always solid *Blue Comet* livery. Note the use of a standard CRRNJ baggage car following the locomotive and tender. (Photograph by George Votava, courtesy of Joel Rosenbaum and Tom Gallo.)

The *Blue Comet* G-3 Pacific No. 832 speeds through the Pine Barrens of southern New Jersey with a full consist. When in motion the locomotive, painted in its blue "livery," followed by its blue consist with a Jersey cream stripe, represented a comet streaking through space. The Pine Barrens was also the home of the legendary Jersey Devil, a dragon-like creature first reported in Lenape Indian folklore. (Courtesy of Joel Rosenbaum and Tom Gallo.)

The *Blue Comet* train is seen building up steam as it departs the Jersey City Terminal with the skyline of New York City, cloaked in an early morning haze, standing majestically in the background. The locomotive is the G-3 Pacific No. 833. The photograph was taken in 1935. (Courtesy of author's collection.)

The *Blue Comet* train is seen here leaving Atlantic City from the Reading Company's Atlantic City Railroad and the Pennsylvania Railroad's West Jersey and Seashore Lines (PRSL) Union Terminal. The train is led by engine No. 832. (Courtesy of author's collection.)

The creation of the Pennsylvania-Reading Seashore Lines in 1933 adversely affected *Blue Comet* ticket sales at the Union Terminal in Atlantic City, as well as in the loss of rail service as the PRR gained a controlling interest in the track from Winslow Junction to Atlantic City. In addition, the PRR, with its convenient mid-city New York Pennsylvania (Penn) Station, was able to provide more direct and frequent rail service to Atlantic City. The *Blue Comet* would make its final run on September 27, 1941, as the end of the depression brought back prosperity and with it an expansion in New Jersey's public highway system and a boom in the private ownership of automobiles. The G-3 Pacific locomotive No. 831 is seen in this photograph in the Jersey City Terminal ready to make the final run of the *Blue Comet* service to Atlantic City. To add insult to injury, the *Blue Comet* sign has been removed from the front of the locomotive below the Elesco feedwater heater. (Courtesy of Joel Rosenbaum and Tom Gallo.)

ᵀʰᵉ Bullet!

Jersey Central's Newest Train

Goes on November 7ᵗʰ

New Jersey Central

It's the "Big Shot"

between **Wilkes-Barre - Allentown Bethlehem - Easton** *and* **New York City ~**

Sharing Track 10 at the CRRNJ Terminal was the short-lived CRRNJ train *Bullet* (1929–1931). The *Bullet* ran from Jersey City to Wilkes-Barre, Pennsylvania. It was designed to compete with the Lehigh Valley's *Black Diamond* train. Since the *Black Diamond* had the luxury of running directly into Penn Station in New York City, and the *Bullet* reached New York City via the ferry connection at Jersey City, the outcome was almost preordained. The *Bullet* started its passenger service on November 7, 1929, and ended service on July 12, 1931. The following image announces the inauguration of the *Bullet* service. The locomotive No. 834 is shown in the center of the montage. (Courtesy of author's collection.)

In the early 1930s, the Baldwin Locomotive Works in Philadelphia, Pennsylvania, was commissioned to build a total of five class G-3 Pacific-type 4-6-2 locomotives for the CRRNJ. These locomotives were numbered 831-835. Locomotive Nos. 831, 832, and 833 were painted in a combination of Packard blue and royal blue and would be used in the *Blue Comet* service. No. 834 was painted Olive Green for service on the CRRNJ *Bullet* train. The No. 835 was painted black and was usually assigned to the *Queen of the Valley* and the *Harrisburg Special* trains. The *Bullet* train, led by CRRNJ's engine No. 834, is seen in this photograph heading westbound at Bayonne, New Jersey. (Courtesy of author's collection.)

Historic Dwellings
and Modern Homes
Side by Side

Miles and Miles of Splendid Scenery

The Bullet traverses a region of surpassing loveliness and great historic interest over one of the finest roadbeds in America~

Every Turn Presents a New Picture

A Pastoral Scene

A Stretch of Rock-ballasted Roadway

For Miles Beside the Old Canal— Still in Service

Despite its apparent barriers to success, the CRRNJ did its very best to promote its newest passenger service as seen in this advertisement which shows various landscapes and picturesque scenes that could be seen by the travelers utilizing its service. (Courtesy of author's collection.)

The Bullet

DINING CAR SERVICE

On the Dining Car attached to "The Bullet" inexpensive Club Breakfasts are served.

Club Breakfasts at 60c to $1.00

Special Club Breakfast including Fruit or Cereal, Miller's Farm Sausage, Fried Apple, Wheat or Buckwheat Cakes, Pure Maple Syrup, Muffins, Toast and Coffee—$1.00.

A la Carte service at popular prices.

Courteous dining room attendants serve you quietly, efficiently and quickly.

If you have never availed yourself of this service do so now and you will find it an added pleasure of traveling on this line.

To Our Guests:—

WE desire to assist our patrons with their travel problems. If I can personally arrange for Pullman accommodations for your return trip, or to points beyond New York, it will be a pleasure to have you avail yourself of my services.

T. J. GAFFNEY, *Conductor.*

"THE BULLET"

The CRRNJ's *Bullet* train provided dining car service, which offered a sumptuous and hearty breakfast for $1. Pullman service was also available along its route. (Courtesy of author's collection.)

5-13 P.M.
QUEEN OF THE VALLEY
BOUND BROOK
SOMERVILLE
RARITAN
NORTH BRANCH
WHITE HOUSE
LEBANON, N.J.
ANNANDALE
HIGH BRIDGE
GLEN GARDNER
HAMPTON
PHILLIPSBURG
EASTON
BETHLEHEM
ALLENTOWN
READING
LEBANON, PENN.
HERSHEY
HARRISBURG

The Reading Company's *Queen of the Valley* was found on Track 12 in the CRRNJ Terminal. It operated in conjunction with the CRRNJ. Designated as train No. 199 westward, it departed daily from the Jersey City Terminal at 5:13 p.m. and arrived at Harrisburg, Pennsylvania at 10:14 p.m. Eastward, it was designated as train No. 192, departing daily from Harrisburg at 8:05 a.m. and arriving back at the Jersey City Terminal at 12:35 p.m. (Courtesy of author's collection.)

The *Queen of the Valley* is seen in this photograph departing Elizabethport, New Jersey, in June 1936. It is headed by the CRRNJ steam locomotive No. 833. As revenue began to wane for the *Blue Comet* service to Atlantic City, the CRRNJ began to use engines originally slated for this particular service to more "profitable" venues such as the *Queen of the Valley* runs. Notice that the "Blue Comet" name on locomotive No. 833 has been removed. (Courtesy of author's collection.)

The *Queen of the Valley* provided a dining club car from New York to Harrisburg, as well as coaches in both directions. This photograph shows the Reading Company 4-6-2 steam locomotive No. 211 traveling eastbound, leading the *Queen of the Valley* east of Freemansburg, Pennsylvania, near where Sculac Road meets Wilson Avenue, in about 1950. (Courtesy of the Donald W. Furler collection, Center for Railroad Photography and Art.)

The *Queen* had the longest sustained continuous record of passenger service at the CRRNJ Terminal, lasting from 1902 until 1963. The train took about 4.5 hours to traverse the 179.5-mile (288.9 km) route from Jersey City, New Jersey, to Harrisburg, Pennsylvania. This photograph was taken in July 1956. (Courtesy of author's collection.)

Sharing Track 12 at the CRRNJ Terminal was the Reading Company's *Harrisburg Special*. Once again, it operated in affiliation with the CRRNJ. It followed the same route as the *Queen of the Valley* from Jersey City to Harrisburg. However, whereas the *Queen* left the CRRNJ Terminal in the early evening, the *Harrisburg Special* operated on an early morning schedule. Westward, the train No. 193 left the Jersey City Terminal daily at 9:04 a.m. and arrived in Harrisburg at 1:45 p.m. Eastward, the train No. 194 left Harrisburg at 4:15 p.m. and arrived back in Jersey City at 9:45 p.m. This photograph shows the CRRNJ's *Blue Comet* Pacific-style locomotive No. 832 hauling the *Harrisburg Special* on October 5, 1938. As previously observed, the CRRNJ transferred its engines to more profitable routes as the popularity of the *Blue Comet* train began to wane in the late 1930s. (Courtesy of author's collection.)

Just like the *Queen of the Valley*, *the Harrisburg Special* provided a dining club car and coaches on its entire route, and in both directions, between New York and Harrisburg. Once again, we see locomotive No. 832 hauling the *Harrisburg Special* train No. 193, this time in a winter setting. This photograph was taken in Bethlehem, Pennsylvania, on February 3, 1940. (Courtesy of author's collection.)

The *Harrisburg Special* never achieved the popularity of the *Queen of the Valley*, and its years of operation at the CRRNJ Terminal only lasted from 1910 to 1955. The train names for both the *Harrisburg Special* and the *Queen of the Valley* were dropped from the timetables in 1953, but the trains themselves continued to run. This photograph shows the Reading Company 4-6-2 steam locomotive No. 214 pulling westbound passenger train No. 193, the *Harrisburg Special*, at Allentown, Pennsylvania, on July 18, 1948. (Courtesy of the Donald W. Furler collection, Center for Railroad Photography and Art.)

Track 19 at the CRRNJ Terminal was the residence of the Reading Company's *Williamsporter* train. And, once again, it operated in affiliation with the CRRNJ, which provided considerable rail linkage for this particular train. The train used the CRRNJ track from Tamaqua, Pennsylvania, to Jersey City. The *Williamsporter's* first run was on January 27, 1930, and its last run was on February 28, 1945. The train's consist included a thorough Pullman sleeper, baggage cars, coaches, and a smoking car. The sleeping car service was discontinued sometime in 1932, but the other through equipment remained until the last run. For the Reading Company, the *Williamsporter* trains' handling of mail and express was considered more important than the passenger business. The train left the Jersey City terminal, traveling westbound, at 12:02 a.m., after transporting its passengers to the terminal from the CRRNJ's Liberty Street ferry terminal at 11:50 p.m. (Courtesy of author's collection.)

The tenure of the *Williamsporter* at the CRRNJ terminal was comparatively short-term; however, the train had one very notable event happen to it during its run. Traveling southbound on Thursday, January 30, 1936, at 11:48 p.m., locomotive No. 610, hauling train No. 14 with its consist of six cars, crashed through the Blue Hill end of the Susquehanna River Bridge at Clement, near Sunbury, Pennsylvania. The accident killed three people and injured thirty people. According to the subsequent accident investigation report, released on April 3, 1936, by the Interstate Commerce Commission, the cause of the accident was excessive speed on a sharp curve. The photograph above shows the locomotive No. 610 partially buried in the embankment while the photograph below shows some of the train's consist resting along the banks of the river after it crashed through the bridge, propelled and led by the locomotive itself. The six-car consist involved in this accident included one combination mail and baggage car, one coach, one combination coach and smoking car, one express car, and two refrigerator cars. (Both, courtesy of the Reading Company Technical and Historical Society.)

The *Williamsporter* provided nighttime passenger service between Jersey City and Williamsport, departing these locations in the wee hours of the morning. Engine No. 610, which was involved in the 1936 crash, was but one of ten wheel configuration 4-6-0C camelback locomotives built by the Reading Company shops in 1910. Nos. 606-615 were patterned after the four originally built in 1905 for the Reading Company by Baldwin (Nos. 602–605). In this photograph, a Reading Company 4-6-0C camelback type steam locomotive No. 613 can be seen pulling a westbound passenger train No. 195 in June 1939 at Allentown, Pennsylvania. Whether or not this is truly a photograph of Reading Company *Williamsporter* is subject to debate, but it is probably a good approximation of what it would have looked like in the daytime hours. (Courtesy of the Donald W. Furler collection, Center for Railroad Photography and Art.)

Three

POST-RAILROAD SERVICE, 1967 TO THE PRESENT

The CRRNJ continued to have financial crises and filed for final bankruptcy in 1967, closing the terminal in Jersey City on April 30. In 1968, the terminal complex was purchased with state and federal funding. In April 1967, the opening of the Aldene Connection led to the end of passenger service to the station and the diverting of all remaining passenger trains to Penn Station in Newark. The terminal was closed, but Hollywood would give it a moment of glory.

The terminal got a shot of needed advertisement and notice when segments of the terminal prominently appeared in the movie *Funny Girl* in 1968.

In 1976, the CRRNJ became part of the Consolidated Rail Corporation (Conrail). In the brief nine years from when the terminal was closed and 1976, the terminal became what one observer describes as a dead space. Fortunately, local residents and activists Morris Pesin and Audrey Zapp, appalled by this decay and waste, convinced the state and federal governments to preserve the terminal with the development of Liberty State Park. Restoration of the terminal led to ferry service beginning once again to the city, Ellis Island, and the Statute of Liberty.

The Liberty State Park and the CRRNJ Terminal played numerous roles in the events of September 11, 2001, and its aftermath. During the attacks, Jersey City residents and office workers gathered and watched in horror the burning and eventual collapse of the Twin Towers. Soon after, dozens of private, commercial, and Coast Guard boats shuttled evacuees from lower Manhattan to the docks at the terminal in the largest boatlift ever undertaken in our history. In the wake of the attacks, New Jersey erected several Remembrance Walls in the terminal building. In the following days and weeks, volunteers manned the New Jersey Family Assistance Center where visitors were welcome to leave notes, pictures, flowers, candles, and other mementos of their shared grief.

The terminal took a severe hit from Mother Nature when Superstorm Sandy slammed into it on October 29, 2012, and flooded the building, breaking windows, and damaging the roof. Interior furnishings, finishes, and utility systems were also damaged. These repairs were made and ferry service to Ellis Island and the Statute of Liberty was soon restored and continues to this day, celebrating The Historic Trilogy of the CRRNJ Terminal, the Statute of Liberty, and Ellis Island.

In 1968, the CRRNJ Terminal doubled for the Baltimore & Ohio Railroad's famed Mount Royal Train Station in these particular scenes shot for the movie *Funny Girl*. These two scenes from the movie itself show the waiting room at the CRRNJ Terminal from different perspectives. The photograph above shows the waiting room with Fanny Brice, portrayed by Barbra Streisand, descending the stairs in the rear; while the photograph below shows the same waiting room from her perspective as she views it from the stairs. The elaborate costumes worn by the cast in this scene were representative of the ornate and glamorous apparel worn by the performers of the *Ziegfeld Follies* in about 1910. Unit production manager Paul Helmick explained, "With the Jersey Central Railroad in bankruptcy and inactive, I found it quite easy to make a deal for use of the ornate, turn-of-the-century train station where Pullman cars were already on the tracks." A bit of trivia, the CRRNJ Terminal in Jersey City stood in for Philadelphia's Reading Terminal in the 1960 movie *From the Terrace*. (Both, courtesy of author's collection.)

The photograph above shows Fanny Brice purchasing a railroad ticket to New York City at the ticket window in the waiting room at the CRRNJ Terminal. Naturally, it is a ticket on the Baltimore & Ohio Railroad. Actress Anne Francis stands to her right in this scene from the movie. The bottom photograph shows the train shed at the terminal as seen in the movie. Beginning in 1967, the tracks were removed from the train shed, but in 1968 some tracks were still around when filming for the movie was done. The tracks were removed in stages over the next decade. By the early 1980s, there were no more tracks on the property. In some areas, the tracks were lifted and sold by CRRNJ, but a lot of trackage was vandalized and stolen. The *Funny Girl* Company was transported by excursion boats from their Manhattan hotel near the cruise ship piers to the New Jersey dock near the train station, avoiding the Holland Tunnel, traffic, and ground transportation. (Both, courtesy of author's collection.)

This is a view of the terminal lobby in the CRRNJ Terminal about a decade after it was closed in 1967. Broken windows, sagging ceilings, flooded floors, paint peeling, rusty frames and trestles, debris everywhere, and the list goes on. (Courtesy of the Library of Congress.)

As Mother Nature reclaimed the ground it once possessed before the era of railroading briefly claimed it as its own, the glorious train shed once filled with tracks of waiting trains, platforms filled with commuters, and distant travelers soon became overgrown with weeds. (Courtesy of author's collection.)

This is a 1987 photograph taken from the north side of the CRRNJ Terminal by an amateur railroad photographer. It is a sunny day, and tourists are beginning to descend on the terminal. The picture was taken by a local gentleman who took many railroad photographs across the nation beginning in the 1960s and up until the 1980s. He had a tripod and took several similar photographs of the same scene, as he sometimes drove a long way to take his beloved railroad images. (Courtesy of author's collection.)

A ferry transports dazed, bewildered, and injured people from the Battery Park Ferry Terminal in lower Manhattan to the wharves at the CRRNJ Terminal. It is September 11, 2001. The Twin Towers at the World Trade Center have just collapsed following a terrorist attack. As people are treated on the grounds of the CRRNJ Terminal, others watch in horror at the surreal scene happening before their eyes just across the Hudson River. (Courtesy of the *Jersey Journal*.)

The *Tribute in Light* is an art installation created in remembrance of the September 11 terrorist attacks in New York City. It consists of 88 vertical searchlights arranged in two columns of light to represent the original World Trade Twin Towers. It stands six blocks from the original World Trade Center on top of the Battery Parking Garage in lower Manhattan. The tradition was begun in early 2002 but has been an annual event on September 11 of every year since then. On a clear night, the lights can be seen from 60 miles away, including all of New York City and most of suburban Northern New Jersey and Long Island. This surrealistically beautiful photograph was taken from the south side of the CRRNJ Terminal on September 11, 2020. (Courtesy of author's collection.)

Hurricane Sandy, also known as Superstorm Sandy, was an extremely destructive and strong Atlantic Ocean hurricane. It was the largest Atlantic hurricane on record as measured by diameter, with tropical storm winds spanning 1,150 miles. It formed on October 2, 2012, and dissipated on November 2, 2012. It greatly affected the entire Caribbean Region with damaging winds and flooding. In the United States, Hurricane Sandy affected 24 states, including the entire eastern seaboard from Florida to Maine, with particularly severe damage in New Jersey and New York. It was a Category 1–equivalent extratropical cyclone off the coast of the northeastern United States. Its storm surge hit New York City on October 29, flooding streets, tunnels, and subway lines, and cutting power in and around the city. It crippled the entire transportation infrastructure in New York City and northern New Jersey. (Courtesy of the National Weather Service.)

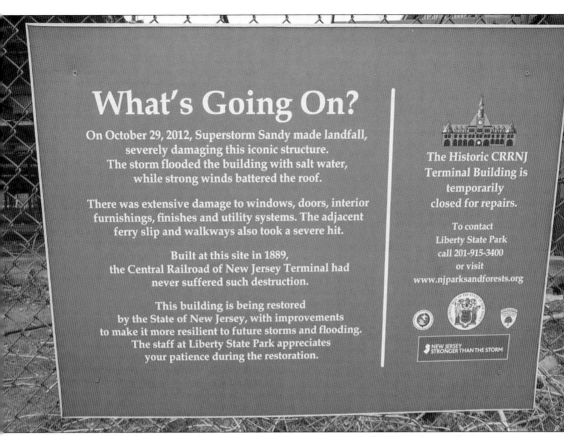

What's Going On?

On October 29, 2012, Superstorm Sandy made landfall,
severely damaging this iconic structure.
The storm flooded the building with salt water,
while strong winds battered the roof.

There was extensive damage to windows, doors, interior
furnishings, finishes and utility systems. The adjacent
ferry slip and walkways also took a severe hit.

Built at this site in 1889,
the Central Railroad of New Jersey Terminal had
never suffered such destruction.

This building is being restored
by the State of New Jersey, with improvements
to make it more resilient to future storms and flooding.
The staff at Liberty State Park appreciates
your patience during the restoration.

The Historic CRRNJ
Terminal Building is
temporarily
closed for repairs.

To contact
Liberty State Park
call 201-915-3400
or visit
www.njparksandforests.org

NEW JERSEY
STRONGER THAN THE STORM

Superstorm Sandy had a profound effect on the CRRNJ Terminal, closing it for nearly four years while repairs were made. This sign described the type of damage done to the building and its adjoining support facilities. (Courtesy of jerseydigs.com.)

Typical of this type of damage inflicted by the passage of Superstorm Sandy was the destruction of the park benches located right in front of the CRRNJ Terminal. Notice the unfinished One World Trade Center building in Manhattan in the background, which replaced the fallen Twin Towers. (Courtesy of author's collection.)

The storm surge caused by Superstorm Sandy flooded the train shed at the CRRNJ Terminal, undulating the site of the former tracks throughout the shed. (Courtesy of jerseydigs.com.)

The hurricane-force winds of Superstorm Sandy wreaked havoc on the roof and tower of the CRRNJ Terminal. Hundreds of roof tiles were blown off, and the copula was severely damaged and had to be replaced. The damage to the terminal and its surrounding facilities cost $18 million to repair and restore. After nearly four years of being closed, finally, on Wednesday, April 20, 2016, the terminal was reopened to the public. (Courtesy of the Library of Congress.)

This photograph of the north side of the CRRNJ Terminal was beautifully captured by Mitchell Dakelman. It is early morning and people are just beginning to mill about the terminal. The skyline of New York City can be seen in the background across the Hudson River. The three-story eclectic Richardson Romanesque–style terminal opened in 1889 and was built by Peabody & Stearns of Boston. The exterior structure was characterized by a steep-pitched roof with dormers on the third floor, prominent arched windows, a cupola, and a tower with a clock facing the waterfront. The interior included a concourse, ticket office, and waiting room of English buff-colored, glazed brick walls on the first floor. The ceiling of the waiting room was supported by red, iron trusses in a starburst design. (Courtesy of Mitchell Dakelman.)

The renewed hustle and noise of people in the concourse is captured in this photograph taken on April 1, 2010, as families with their children explore the many attractions of the CRRNJ Terminal. (Courtesy of author's collection.)

The waiting room in the CRRNJ Terminal welcomes toddlers and young children to the wonders of a once-forgotten and unappreciated part of railroad history in America. (Courtesy of author's collection.)

This magnificent view of the CRRNJ Terminal was taken from the top of One World Trade Center in Lower Manhattan. The terminal is now part of the Liberty State Park complex. (Courtesy of author's collection.)

This almost surreal photograph of the CRRNJ Terminal was beautifully captured by Steven Dingman. Mr. Dingman took the photograph while aboard a ferry traveling from Liberty Harbor. Liberty Harbor is a neighborhood in Jersey City, New Jersey, situated on the Morris Canal Big Basin opposite Liberty State Park. The buildings in the immediate background are in Liberty Harbor. (Courtesy of Steven Dingman.)

The interior of the CRRNJ Terminal includes the information desk and the waiting room. The ceiling is supported by red, iron trusses in a brilliant starburst design. (Courtesy of the author's collection.)

Four

KEEPING THE MEMORY
OF THE TERMINAL ALIVE

The CRRNJ Terminal has a number of historical plaques, displays, and markers that tell the story of its past from its beginning, its role in American history, its endurance in the face of natural and manmade disasters, its contribution to the history of railroading, and its role in the rail transportation within the state of New Jersey. In addition to these remembrances, there is a monument dedicated to the hardworking and devoted employees of the CRRNJ, who were the backbone of the railroad from 1949 to 1976. These remembrances are located at the terminal and its surrounding grounds.

Numerous fairs, historic interpretative programs, concerts, and other sponsored events have taken place within the station and its grounds. Among them are the May 1991 train show hosted by ex-CRRNJ employee Walter Matuch; the September 2003 event cosponsored by the CRRNJ Veteran Organization and the Liberty State Park, honoring veterans of the CRRNJ Railroad and the Heritage; and the All Points West Music & Arts Festivals.

In addition, the personnel at the Liberty State Park have hosted a number of yearly and monthly events recalling the significance and contribution of the CRRNJ Terminal, notably in regard to the *Blue Comet* train and the terminal's unique role as part of The Historic Trilogy. Lectures and interpretative presentations are conducted in the terminal's Blue Comet Auditorium.

Besides all of this history, the terminal itself has been preserved for future generations to appreciate its architectural exquisiteness and the remembrance of a bygone era of elegance, grace, and beauty for all to embrace and cherish. Tours are conducted on a regular basis, and highlight the terminal's architectural innovation, uniqueness, and heritage.

All of these remembrances and events are intended to keep the public aware of the unique contribution and heritage of the terminal as the "Gateway to America." The terminal was a grand setting for much of New Jersey's transportation history in the northeast, and the home of some of the most famous trains in the history of American railroading.

"There's a real nostalgia here, not only with the train shed but also with the interior. It is quite beautiful and it is of an era that's gone by, so there's a past that we have to appreciate, respect, and preserve," said Janet Akhtarshenas, a historical interpreter at Liberty State Park.

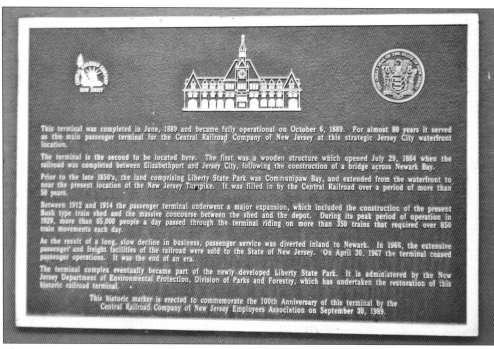

This terminal was completed in June, 1889 and became fully operational on October 6, 1889. For almost 80 years it served as the main passenger terminal for the Central Railroad Company of New Jersey at this strategic Jersey City waterfront location.

The terminal is the second to be located here. The first was a wooden structure which opened July 29, 1864 when the railroad was completed between Elizabethport and Jersey City, following the construction of a bridge across Newark Bay.

Prior to the late 1850's, the land comprising Liberty State Park was Communipaw Bay, and extended from the waterfront to near the present location of the New Jersey Turnpike. It was filled in by the Central Railroad over a period of more than 50 years.

Between 1912 and 1914 the passenger terminal underwent a major expansion, which included the construction of the present Bush type train shed and the massive concourse between the shed and the depot. During its peak period of operation in 1929, more than 65,000 people a day passed through the terminal riding on more than 350 trains that required over 850 train movements each day.

As the result of a long, slow decline in business, passenger service was diverted inland to Newark. In 1966, the extensive passenger and freight facilities of the railroad were sold to the State of New Jersey. On April 30, 1967 the terminal ceased passenger operations. It was the end of an era.

The terminal complex eventually became part of the newly developed Liberty State Park. It is administered by the New Jersey Department of Environmental Protection, Division of Parks and Forestry, which has undertaken the restoration of this historic railroad terminal.

This historic marker is erected to commemorate the 100th Anniversary of this terminal by the Central Railroad Company of New Jersey Employees Association on September 30, 1989.

The Central Railroad of New Jersey Terminal Marker is located in front of the CRRNJ Terminal. Part of the inscription on the plaque reads as follows: "This terminal was completed in June 1889, and became fully operational on October 6, 1889. For almost 80 years, it served as the main passenger terminal for the Central Railroad Company of New Jersey at this strategic Jersey City waterfront location." This marker was erected by the Central Railroad Company of New Jersey Employees Association on September 30, 1989, to commemorate the 100th anniversary of this terminal. (Courtesy of Mitchell Dakelman.)

The Central New Jersey Employees Monument was designed by Sam Myers and Bob Hoeft, both past CNJ Veteran Association Presidents. The engravings are simple and poignant: the number zero is on all four sides of the milepost, signifying the beginning of the line. The central block reads, "Honoring the Employees of the Central Railroad of New Jersey 1849-1976." The CNJ heralds appear on the sides of the base. On the center of the base is engraved, "Dedicated by the Central Railroad of New Jersey Veteran Employees Association." (Courtesy of Mitchell Dakelman.)

The Historic Trilogy

The term "Historic Trilogy" is used to represent the role the Central Railroad of New Jersey (CRRNJ) Terminal, Ellis Island and the Statue of Liberty played in American history. It was these three historic structures that greeted most of the immigrants arriving to the New York Harbor area during the wave of immigration of the 19th and early 20th centuries.

The Statue of Liberty, dedicated in 1886, was a gift from the people of France to the people of the United States. Its original intent was to symbolize a common belief in democracy. It quickly became an universal symbol of hope and freedom, especially to those immigrants fleeing political and religious persecution in Europe and the Soviet Union.

The Ellis Island Immigration Station opened in 1892 to process the 12 million immigrants pouring into the New York Harbor area. These people supplied the labor, and in some cases the expertise, which fueled the industrial revolution in this country. Today, over half of the people living in the U.S. can trace their ancestry back to those immigrants.

Completing the trilogy is the CRRNJ Terminal. Constructed in 1889, it was expanded to its current dimension in 1914, due to increased rail and ferry traffic. Besides transporting hundreds of thousands of commuters to New York City, the Terminal was used by about two thirds of the immigrants processed on Ellis Island, finding their way to a new life.

The CRRNJ Terminal, the cornerstone of Liberty State Park, provides us with a concrete connection to the past. Listed on both the State and National Register of Historic Places, its association with the Statue of Liberty and Ellis Island remind us of our distinctive past.

The Historic Trilogy display is located in front of the CRRNJ Terminal. The term "Historic Trilogy" is used to represent the role the Central Railroad of New Jersey (CRRNJ) Terminal, Ellis Island, and the Statue of Liberty played in American history. It was these three historic structures that greeted most of the immigrants arriving in the New York Harbor area during the wave of immigration of the 19th and early 20th centuries. (Both, courtesy of Mitchell Dakelman.)

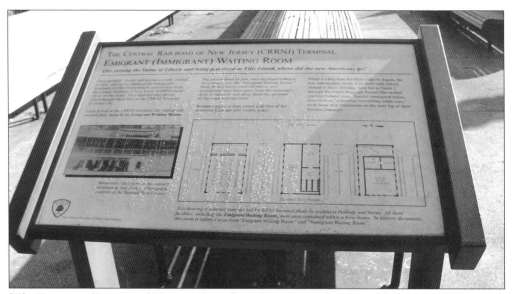

"The Emigrant (Immigrant) Waiting Room" marker is located in front of the CRRNJ Terminal. The Inscription on the marker reads as follows: "After passing the Statue of Liberty and being processed at Ellis Island, where did the new Americans go?" Almost two-thirds of the immigrants processed at Ellis Island bought train tickets from the Central Railroad of New Jersey ticket office on the island. A photograph of newly arrived immigrants appears on the left of the marker with the caption, "Immigrants ride a ferry to the railroad terminals in New Jersey." (Courtesy of Mitchell Dakelman.)

This marker is also located in the front of the CRRNJ Terminal. The marker reads as follows: "Ferry Houses: Connecting People, Boats and Trains / From 1864 until 1967: the Central Railroad of New Jersey (CRRNJ) Terminal provided a vital link between the New Jersey and New York City shores. At its busiest, more than 200 ferry sailings transported tens of thousands of commuters and thousands of immigrants over the New York Harbor waters every day." (Courtesy of Mitchell Dakelman.)

Empty Sky is the official New Jersey September 11 memorial to the state's victims of the 9/11 terrorist attacks on the United States. It is located in Liberty State Park near the CRRNJ Terminal and the site where ferries from lower Manhattan brought the injured from the attacks to a staging area. Designed by Jessica Jamroz and Frederic Schwartz, *Empty Sky* was dedicated on Saturday, September 10, 2011, a day before the 10th anniversary of the attacks. The memorial is dedicated to 746 New Jerseyans killed in the World Trade Center in 1993, and in the September 11 attacks, as well as those who died on September 11, 2001, at the Pentagon and in Shanksville, Pennsylvania. The memorial includes twin walls transecting a gently sloped mound, anchored by a granite path that is directed toward Ground Zero. The names of each of the 746 victims are etched in stainless steel letters. The photograph below shows the twin walls with the towering One World Trade Center building in the background. (Both, courtesy of author's collection.)

The CRRNJ Terminal is a very popular site for viewing the annual Fourth of July fireworks display. If there's one fireworks show to see when you are in New York City, it's the Macy's Fourth of July Fireworks Show. It is one of the most iconic fireworks displays in the United States. Each Fourth of July beginning just after 9:00 p.m., the skies over New York City's East River light up with a colorful, coordinated display. Sponsored by Macy's, there are more than 60,000 shells launched off from between four and six barges. For over 25 minutes, one can enjoy a celebration of America's Independence Day. Not to be missed is the New York Fire Department's contribution, as they shoot red, clear, and blue water 300 feet into the air from the fire boats they have stationed in the river too. It is an annual celebration of both the United States and the unique contribution of the CRRNJ Terminal to our nation's history and heritage. The following photographs show visitors purchasing souvenirs on July 4, 1992, inside the terminal, and then in awe, watching the fireworks display from outside the train shed. (Both, courtesy of Mitchell Dakelman.)

The Central Railroad of New Jersey has hosted a number of heritage festivals over the years. These festivals have included, for instance, memorabilia, displays, and lectures regarding railroad history in New Jersey, as well as honoring the ethnic contributions and heritage of various nationalities. This particular heritage festival pays tribute to the rich, ethnic heritage of the Orient and its people. It included games, displays, lectures, interactive demonstrations, food vendors, and fun for all ages. The festival was held in the Waiting Room area of the CRRNJ Terminal. (Courtesy of author's collection.)

The Liberty State Park has held various open houses at the CRRNJ Terminal. These open houses are intended to inform the general public about the rich history and heritage of the terminal over the years. These include displays and exhibits regarding the *Blue Comet*, the history of the terminal itself, and historic events that occurred near the terminal, such as the Black Tom explosion. This particular open house was held on August 14, 2010. (Both, courtesy of author's collection.)

The very popular Blue Comet Days were held from 2018 through 2020 at the Liberty State Park's CRRNJ Terminal. They were highlighted by the 2009 release of the documentary film *Deluxe: The Tale of the Blue Comet*, produced by famed New Jersey filmmaker and historian Robert A. Emmons. The Blue Comet Day held on Saturday, February 24, 2018, featured a screening of the film in the Blue Comet Auditorium, as well as a children's workshop and craft program about trains, including displays and memorabilia dealing with the Blue Comet train, all of which were presented in the waiting room area of the terminal. (Both, courtesy of author's collection.)

Blue Comet Day

Saturday, February 24th, 2018 10:00 AM – 3:00 PM
Liberty State Park CRRNJ Terminal
FREE

In celebration of the 89th anniversary of the inaugural run of the Blue Comet train, join us at the Central Railroad of New Jersey Terminal for Blue Comet Day! Journey back in time to learn about the trail of the famous Blue Comet train all the way to its final destination of Atlantic City.

10:00 AM – 11:00 AM All Aboard! - A children's program, which will include a talk about trains and a take home craft. This program is appropriate for ages 5 to 10 years old. Pre-registration is required, and all children must be accompanied by an adult for the duration of the program.

12:00 PM – 1:30 PM Trail of the Blue Comet - This program will include a discussion about the lasting impact of the Blue Comet, artifacts from the train, and a clip from the documentary, "Deluxe: The Tale of the Blue Comet." No pre-registration is required.

1:30 PM – 3:00 PM "Deluxe: The Tale of the Blue Comet." - A showing of Robert A. Emmons Jr.'s 90-minute documentary in the Blue Comet Auditorium. No pre-registration is required.

For more information about Blue Comet Day or to register for the All Aboard! program, please contact the Nature Interpretive Center at 201-915-3400 x202 or email LSPNatureCenter@dep.nj.gov.

Blue Comet Day

Saturday, February 23rd, 2019
10:00 AM - 3:00 PM
FREE; *Pre-registration required for childrens'*
program only.
Please call or email to register

*In celebration of the 90th anniversary of the inaugural run of the Blue Comet
train, join us at the Central Railroad of New Jersey Terminal for Blue Comet
Day! Journey back in time to learn about the trail of the famous Blue Comet all
the way to its final destination of Atlantic City*

Schedule of the day's events:

10:00 AM – 11:00 AM All Aboard! A children's program which will include a
discussion and a train craft. This program is appropriate for ages 5 to 10 years old.
Pre-registration is required, and all children must be accompanied by an adult for the
duration of the program.
10:45 AM - 11:15 AM Anthony Puzzilla, author of *New Jersey Central's Blue Comet*,
will speak about the February 21st, 1929 inaugural run of the Blue Comet train and
be available for a Q&A session. Copies of his book will be available for purchase.
11:30 AM – 12:15 PM Frank T. Reilly, president of the CNJ Historical
Society and author of *The Blue Comet: Its Exciting History and First Person
Accounts*, will showcase a PowerPoint presentation about the iconic train.
12:30 PM – 1:15 PM Veterans of the CNJ will speak about their many years of
experience working for the railroad, and will then be available to answer questions.
1:30 PM – 3:00 PM "Deluxe: The Tale of the Blue Comet." A showing of Robert A.
Emmons Jr.'s 90-minute documentary in the Blue Comet
Auditorium.

The Blue Comet Day held on Saturday, February 23, 2019, celebrated the 90th anniversary of the inaugural run of the *Blue Comet* train on February 21, 1929. The author made a presentation regarding this anniversary in the Blue Comet Auditorium. In addition, a children's workshop and train craft program was held in the waiting room area of the CRRNJ Terminal, along with various displays, exhibits, and models pertaining to the *Blue Comet* train. Also, there was the traditional showing of the documentary film *Deluxe: The Tale of the Blue Comet*. There was also a presentation by Frank T. Reilly talking about the iconic train, followed by an open discussion by former Central Railroad of New Jersey employees talking about their own personal experiences working for the railroad. (Both, courtesy of author's collection.)

The Blue Comet Day held on Saturday, February 22, 2020, was a varied program dealing with the Blue Comet train with the traditional children's workshop and craft program about trains and a showing of the film *Deluxe: The Tale of the Blue Comet.* These included a train simulation of a virtual ride on the *Blue Comet* train, and the author's narration of actual movies of the train at the annual American Railway Master Mechanics' Association Convention held in Atlantic City Station in June 1929. In addition, there was a presentation by Frank T. Reilly and an interactive panel discussion led by Tom Gallo regarding experiences of actually working for the Central Railroad of New Jersey in the Blue Comet Auditorium. (Both, courtesy of author's collection.)

Blue Comet Day

Saturday, February 22nd, 2020
10:00 AM – 3:00 PM
Liberty State Park CRRNJ Terminal

In celebration of the 91st anniversary of the inaugural run of The Blue Comet train, join us at the Central Railroad of New Jersey Terminal for Blue Comet Day! Journey back in time to learn about the trail of the famous Blue Comet all the way to its final destination of Atlantic City. Please see the reverse side of this flyer for a schedule of the day's events.

For more information about Blue Comet Day or to register for the All Aboard! program, please contact the Nature Center at 201-915-3400 x202 or email LSPNatureCenter@dep.nj.gov.

Blue Comet Day

10:00 AM – 10:45 AM All Aboard! A children's program which includes a discussion about trains and a take home craft. This program is recommended for ages 5 to 10 years old. *Pre-registration is required, and all children must be accompanied by an adult for the duration of the program.*

10:45 AM - 11:30 AM A student from Hunterdon County will present, "A Virtual Ride on The Blue Comet," by demonstrating how to use a train simulator app to build The Blue Comet train.

11:30 AM – 12:30 PM Anthony Puzzilla, author of *New Jersey Central's Blue Comet,* will narrate *The Blue Comet Movie,* and also speak about Locomotive 592's special connection with The Blue Comet. Copies of his book will be available for purchase.

12:30 PM – 1:30 PM Frank T. Reilly, president of the CNJ Historical Society and author of *The Blue Comet: Its Exciting History and First Person Accounts,* will showcase a PowerPoint presentation about the iconic train. Tom Gallo, a CNJ veteran employee and author of several books about the CNJ, will then moderate an interactive discussion with veterans of the CNJ, detailing their many years of experience working for the railroad.

1:30 PM – 3:00 PM "Deluxe: The Tale of the Blue Comet." A showing of Robert A. Emmons Jr.'s 90-minute documentary will take place in the Blue Comet Auditorium.

In addition to these activities inside the CRRNJ Terminal being held on February 22, 2020, the train shed was decorated with a number of displays and banners. Track 3 was adorned with posters showing the effects of Superstorm Sandy on the CRRNJ Terminal and its surroundings. The track was also draped with a banner discussing the extensive commuter service provided by the terminal in its heyday, and briefly mentioning that a large number of named trains originated from the terminal over the years, including the *Blue Comet*. Track 10 was draped with a large poster of CRRNJ engineer John V. Wait and conductor Joseph T. Ross proudly posing for a publicity photograph with the *Blue Comet* G-3s Pacific No. 831 at Jersey City Terminal. Engineer Wait and conductor Ross were chosen to make the first revenue run on February 21, 1929. At the time of this photograph, in 1929, Wait and Ross had 53 and 51 years of CRRNJ service respectively. (Courtesy of author's collection.)

The Art Fair 14C found a new location in 2023 at the CRRNJ Terminal at the Liberty State Park. Annually, at different locations in the Jersey City, New Jersey area, the fair provides a showcase for hundreds of artists from New Jersey, New York and around the world giving art lovers exposure to a wide variety of visual arts, of all kinds and for all budgets. The 2023 Art Fair ran from October 12 to 15, 2023, and attracted literally thousands of attendees with 80 exhibition booths. Beginning on October 19, 2024, a new art exhibition will be held in the terminal. It will be entitled "Employees of the CRRNJ" and will honor the dedicated and loyal men and women who were literally the backbone of the railroad. (Courtesy of Art Fair 14C.)

The revitalization of the CRRNJ Train Shed, as part of the Liberty State Park Revitalization Program, will transform the existing ugly and decrepit train shed into a beautiful, family friendly covered and open areas which will contain a tram stop, a railroad and art exhibition, a garden walk, fresh farm produce area, a gathering courtyard and water fountain. (Courtesy of the New Jersey Department of Environmental Protection.)

Discover Thousands of Local History Books
Featuring Millions of Vintage Images

Arcadia Publishing, the leading local history publisher in the United States, is committed to making history accessible and meaningful through publishing books that celebrate and preserve the heritage of America's people and places.

Find more books like this at
www.arcadiapublishing.com

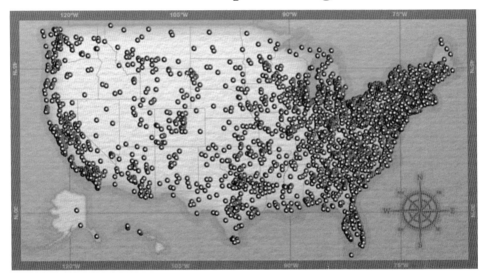

Search for your hometown history, your old stomping grounds, and even your favorite sports team.

Consistent with our mission to preserve history on a local level, this book was printed in South Carolina on American-made paper and manufactured entirely in the United States. Products carrying the accredited Forest Stewardship Council (FSC) label are printed on 100 percent FSC-certified paper.

MADE IN THE
USA